*Dedicated to the memory of my beloved mother,
Mary Sweitzer, who loved and prayed our family into
the kingdom and established a heritage of blessing
for generations yet to come.*
—MARILYN HICKEY

*Dedicated to my mom and mentor.
Thanks for always encouraging, believing, and investing
in me. You have instilled a powerful love for the Bible
in me and have shown me through life how the Bible
can be relevant in a daily way. May we always serve
God's purpose in our generation (Acts 13:36)!*
—SARAH BOWLING

Praise for Marilyn and Sarah

"*BLESSING THE NEXT GENERATION* is an exciting new book that's filled with God's principles of blessing for His people. Marilyn and Sarah point out from God's Word and from their own personal experiences the fact that God wants to save and bless our families. He's called us to raise strong, godly families, and He's told us in His Word how we can do that. This book boldly declares that 'a life built on God's Truth becomes the foundation for generational blessing.'

"Marilyn and Sarah give us wonderful, Bible-based principles that can help us receive and maintain the blessing of God in our lives and pass it along to the generations to come. They believe very strongly that God has a vision for our families, and it's up to each one of us, as believers, to speak that vision into being. And, above all, they point out that we are 'blessed to be a blessing' (Genesis 12:1-3). God desires for us to reach out to others with the good news that He wants to bless them and bless their families!"

—Richard Roberts, president and CEO,
Oral Roberts University

"I would like to wholeheartedly recommend the book titled *BLESSING THE NEXT GENERATION,* by Marilyn Hickey and her daughter, Sarah Bowling. Marilyn Hickey has been a faithful Church Growth International board member for many years, and I have heard her anointed messages concerning generational blessings. Her daughter, Sarah, is a wonderful example of all that her mother teaches. They have lived out what they teach, and they have great expertise in this important area of biblical knowledge. When you read and study this book, you will be able to gain supernatural insight into generational blessings."

—David Yonggi Cho, chairman,
Church Growth International

"This lovely mother-daughter combination of Marilyn and Sarah has blessed the church with one of the most encouraging books to come along in years. We all have skeletons in the closet when it comes to our family tree. *BLESSING THE NEXT GENERATION* can set those free who have thought there was no way forward because of their family traits. It shows how you and I can be an exception in spite of the least-promising background. Reflecting a high view of Scripture, the importance of forgiveness, and gratitude, this book provides a useful formula that shows how you can be emancipated from the worst possible past to become a dazzling trophy of grace for the future."

—Dr. R. T. Kendall, bestselling author and speaker

"In a culture that elevates self to the point where connection with past and future is lost, this book drives home our relationship with those who have gone before and those who are yet to come, highlighting why we are the way we are, practical ways to break free, and the ramifications of our daily life decisions not only for now, but for generations to come. It brings to life the truths of the Word and how to practically apply them so that fear can be turned into faith, and how the ensuing peace of God can bring freedom and how victory. It is excellent, relevant, practical, and challenging."

—Korey & John Cooper,
Contemporary Christian music artists

blessing
the
next generation

Creating *a* Lasting
Family Legacy *with the* Help
of a Loving God

MARILYN HICKEY AND
SARAH BOWLING

Faith
Words

New York Boston Nashville

Unless otherwise indicated, all Scripture quotations are taken from the Holy Bible, New Living Translation, copyright © 1996. Used by permission of Tyndale House Publishers, Inc., Wheaton, IL 60189. All rights reserved.
Scriptures noted AMP are taken from the Amplified® Bible. Copyright © 1954, 1962, 1965, 1987 by The Lockman Foundation. Used by permission.
Scriptures noted KJV are taken from the King James Version of the Bible.
Scriptures noted MSG are taken from The Message. Copyright © 1993, 1994, 1995, 1996, 2000, 2001, 2002. Used by permission of NavPress Publishing Group.
Scriptures noted NIV are taken from the HOLY BIBLE: NEW INTERNATIONAL VERSION®. Copyright © 1973, 1978, 1984 by International Bible Society. Used by permission of Zondervan Publishing House.
All rights reserved.
Scriptures noted NKJV are taken from the NEW KING JAMES VERSION. Copyright © 1979, 1980, 1982, Thomas Nelson, Inc., Publishers.

FaithWords
Hachette Book Group
237 Park Avenue
New York, NY 10017

Visit our Web site at www.faithwords.com.

Printed in the United States of America

First Edition: January 2008
10 9 8 7 6

FaithWords is a division of Hachette Book Group, Inc.
The FaithWords name and logo is a trademark of
Hachette Book Group, Inc.

Library of Congress Cataloging-in-Publication Data

Hickey, Marilyn.
   Blessing the next generation : create a lasting family legacy with the help of a loving God / Marilyn Hickey & Sarah Bowling. — 1st ed.
      p, cm.
   Includes bibliographical references.
   ISBN-13: 978-0-446-69989-1
   ISBN-10: 0-446-69989-6
   1. Family—Religious aspects—Christianity. 2. Family—Religious life.
   3. Spiritual formation. I. Bowling, Sarah. II. Title.
   BT707.7. H52 2007
   248.4—dc22   2007011214

ACKNOWLEDGMENTS

Our thanks to ...

Reverend Jack Hanes, senior pastor, Penrith Christian Life Centre, Sydney, Australia;

The Reverend R.T. Kendall, former senior minister, Westminster Chapel, London, England;

Reverend Joel Osteen, senior pastor, Lakewood Church, Houston, Texas ...

for your dedication in reaching the generations and for your remarkable insights included in this book.

CONTENTS

INTRODUCTION:
CHOOSE THE BEST!

Nobody could understand why Roland was dying. He had experienced a common head cold the previous month but seemingly recovered. Then he began to complain of feeling tired and weak. He took to his bed and in six weeks' time, he weakened to the point that physicians encouraged his close family members to gather and prepare to say good-bye.

One of those who came to Roland's bedside was his long-time friend, Pastor Jim. "I'm here to pray for your healing!" Pastor Jim said boldly.

"Pray that my death will be peaceful," Roland countered.

"Are you sure this is your time to die?" Pastor Jim asked, looking directly into Roland's eyes.

"Yes," Roland replied weakly as he looked away from his friend's penetrating gaze.

"What makes you think so?" Pastor Jim pressed.

"Well," Roland said in slow and measured words, "I'm sixty-seven. My mother died at sixty-seven. I'm just like my mother—I've had all the ailments she had. I've got my mother's genes."

"How old was your father when he died?" Pastor Jim asked.

Roland smiled briefly. "You know Dad is still alive. He's at Crestwood Manor. He's eighty-eight."

"Right!" said Pastor Jim. "Dad's still going strong, isn't he?"

"Yes," Roland said. "He's still playing golf five times a week and going to church every Sunday. He's a real warhorse."

Pastor Jim then said, "I'm going to talk straight to you, Ro. I don't think it's your time to go. I think you still have lots of things to contribute to your family and to this city and to your church—you still have important things to do for God. I am going to pray for your healing, and there's something I am going to insist you do as I pray and after I leave. I'm not going to leave here until you promise me you're going to do what I ask you to do."

"What's that?" Roland asked.

"You've got to start believing for your *father's* genes!"

Roland balked at first but finally agreed, and Pastor Jim prayed.

Roland got out of bed later that afternoon. He got up the next day and got dressed. Within two weeks he had recovered the level of energy and strength he enjoyed two months before his mystery illness. Roland lived for twenty-three years after that day when Pastor Jim prayed at his bedside. He was active in his community, served two terms on his church board, and even went on five overseas short-term missions trips while he was in his seventies and early eighties.

Did Roland experience a miracle healing?

Yes. But the miracle probably was as much emotional and spiritual as it was physical. The truth is, Roland began to believe he could and should and would *live*. He made a choice with his will and his faith. Roland chose to believe for the *best* health and vitality he might experience. *He chose to believe for God's best.*

What about you? Are you truly believing for God's best today?

WHAT ARE YOU BELIEVING GOD FOR?

Don't settle for less than the best. It's easy to think, *I don't deserve any better than this.* It's easy to become discouraged and think, *Things are never going to get any better.* Don't give in to less-than-best thinking!

The Bible is clear. God wants us to experience the best in life, including:

- the best spiritual blessings.
- the best possible physical health.
- the best emotional well-being.
- the best in all our relationships.
- the best in our material lives.

"Best" is going to be a little different for each person, but "best" is the standard God sets!

God gave His best—His only Son, Jesus Christ—so every person who believes in Him and accepts what Jesus did on the cross might have eternal life in heaven, a spiritual life *free of sin* and guilt, and an abundant earthly life overflowing with all things not just good, but *great*! When you accept Jesus, you get the *best*. When you receive the Holy Spirit whom Jesus promised and sent, you get the *best*.

God also gave us the key that unlocks the best in every area of our lives. That key is *faith*. Allow the Scriptures to guide and focus your faith for your family. Here is a beautiful illustration of generational blessing from the book of Psalms:

> Happy are those who fear the LORD.
> Yes, happy are those who delight in doing what he
> commands.
> Their children will be successful everywhere;
> an entire generation of godly people will be blessed.
> They themselves will be wealthy,
> and their good deeds will never be forgotten.
> When darkness overtakes the godly,
> light will come bursting in.
> They are generous, compassionate, and righteous.
> All goes well for those who are generous,
> who lend freely and conduct their business fairly.
> Such people will not be overcome by evil circumstances.
> Those who are righteous will be long remembered.
> They do not fear bad news;
> they confidently trust the LORD to care for them.
> They are confident and fearless and can face their foes
> triumphantly.
> They give generously to those in need.
> Their good deeds will never be forgotten.
> They will have influence and honor.
>
> (PSALM 112:1–9)

Read passages like this one again and again. Share them with your family and speak them in your prayers to God. Before you know it, you will be convinced that *God wants* the best for you and your family—and your faith will cause you to yield to it.

No Matter How Bad It Was . . .

People often talk about the good ol' days.

For many people, the good ol' days are really the bad ol' days. Many people did not grow up in happy homes. They did not have idyllic childhoods. Even today, countless millions of people around the world live in dysfunctional families filled with problems—not only do they have problem-prone parents and problem-saturated siblings, but their extended family members have serious problems. Some people can point to a long line of dysfunction in their families.

And guess what?

Jesus could have said that about the physical family lineage into which He was born! Just look at who and what was in Jesus' family tree:

- Judah and Tamar—an example of incest
- Rahab—a harlot who lived in an enemy city
- Ruth—a Moabite, someone with whom the Israelites were to have no association
- David—who, although he had a heart for God, was a king who committed both adultery and murder
- Solomon—who, rather than trust God, made political alliances that resulted in his having a thousand wives, the support of whom put his nation into bankruptcy
- Amon—who sacrificed to carved idols

The list goes on!

Jesus, however, didn't "live down" to his family's worst reputation—he "lived up" to His heavenly Father's *best*!

IS THE BEST REALLY POSSIBLE?

There are four things we challenge you to believe today:

1. Having God's best isn't something you can accomplish on your own. God's best is accomplished only in partnership with God. This is especially true when it comes to your family. Establishing a godly family and creating a generational blessing that goes on into the future is a supernatural act, not a natural one. It's a matter of faith.

2. God calls us to use both our faith and our wills as we take a long, hard look at our family lives. We must address what is wrong, evil, hurtful, and unproductive—and cast those things from our lives. We do this by an act of our will and faith.

Then we must build into our lives and our families what produces good. Again, we do this *by an act of our wills and our faith.*

3. Anything of lasting and eternal value is developed over time. The only truly eternal thing completed in an "instant" is your acceptance of Jesus Christ as your Savior. With a simple decision, you can be saved in a moment—instantly transformed from an "old creature" to a "new creature." Everything from that moment on—becoming a disciple—is a process over time.

Your mind is renewed over time and by a process.

Your faith grows over time and by a process.

Your walk with the Lord is just that, a process of many steps.

The establishment of God's best in your life is a process that unfolds over time.

That means there's no simple one-two-three formula for having the perfect family, or for living a life free of all pain or hardship. It also means you *can* put in place certain foundation stones on which to build God's best. The devil is defeated in our families as we develop new habits for ourselves and our children.

4. The process of pursuing God's best takes intention. It doesn't happen by accident. The Bible tells us, "As the bird by wandering, as the swallow by flying, so the curse causeless shall not come" (Proverbs 26:2 KJV). In other words, everything has an underlying cause.

We may not understand how or why something has happened, but if we were able to peel back all of the mystery and see as God sees, we would understand that everything has a beginning point—a direct or indirect cause. Everything happens because somebody, somewhere in our past, set certain things in motion.

What exists in your family tree today may have started a generation ago, or several generations ago.

The good news is this, what you do today—right now and in the days to come—can start a new pattern! You can set into motion the habits and "causes" for something great in your future, and in the future of your entire family.

Oh, But You Really Are "Like" Your Family

"Oh, I'm not like my family," some people say, but to a certain extent, you *are* like your family.

You may have been adopted at birth, but you were born into a bloodline—a "birth family"—and what you inherited from that family is a *fact* of your life. Every person is born with a genetic code that is fixed to a great degree. You can change your hair color and wear colored contact lenses to change your eye color, but you can't change your height, bone structure, or your basic personality. Your emotional disposition *can* be changed by God as you respond to Him with your faith. But the fact remains: a large part of who you are was determined before birth. Recognize this important truth as you read the chapters following.

This does not at all diminish the importance of family in God's plan. The family is entirely God's idea. From the first chapters of the Bible, we see God has always been concerned about the family and desired to bless the family. The family was the first organizational unit God put into place—marriage was intended to multiply into family. (See Genesis 2:18, 21–25.)

We've all heard the phrase, "What goes around comes around." How true that is in families! We see ourselves in our children and grandchildren. No doubt our grandparents and parents saw themselves in us!

A family's characteristics tend to become more pronounced over time. A trait becomes entrenched, for good or for bad. Every family tree is becoming more negative or more positive with each generation. God's desire, however, is for your family to be on an upward spiral, and through Him it can be!

When we chart a family tree, we usually make a vertical diagram. We put our ancestors at the top and then chart as many generations as we can. God expects the gospel to be passed down *vertically* through our family.

At the same time, our family is to share the good news of Jesus with others we meet *horizontally*—from neighbor to neighbor, from stranger to stranger, from coworker to coworker, from church member to church member. Whether or not we bear natural children, we can bear spiritual children who are not of our bloodline.

What do you desire? Do you really want all God has for you and your family?

Are you willing to make the changes that will put you into a position to experience God's best?

If your answers are yes, this book is for you!

Insight from Marilyn

My daughter, Sarah, and I are writing this book together. What a blessing it is for me as a mother to have a daughter to work with me in ministry! Sarah and her husband, Reece, have assumed the mantle of leadership at the church my husband, Wally, and I established many years ago in Denver: *Orchard Road Christian Center.* Sarah has traveled with me in ministry to many nations. We have a television program together. How wonderful for us to write *together* a book about generational blessings and to share our experiences as a family.

Sarah and I are in agreement about the teaching of this book, so as you read the chapters that follow, you will be hearing us as one voice for the most part. Even so, each of us has her own distinct personality and experiences. You will find specific comments and sharing from us *individually* in the sections that are identified as "Insights from Marilyn" and "Insights from Sarah."

I thank God for what He is doing in my family and in my relationship with Sarah. I'm not a singer, but if I was, I'd want to sing duets. This book is our duet.

Insight from Sarah

I love to study and experience God's blessings! I am fully convinced that all *true* blessings come from God, and I love to "rehearse" the blessings He gives.

For starters, God places us in families. I feel incredibly blessed to have been placed in my family. I feel especially blessed that my grandmother had a hunger and passion for the Word of God, my mother has that hunger and passion, and now I have that hunger and passion, too.

God gives us health. I feel incredibly blessed to be in good health. I work at staying fit and I enjoy sports. As a family, we do all we can to stay healthy, but ultimately, it is God who heals and brings us to wholeness.

God gives us children. I feel incredibly blessed to have our three children. My husband, Reece, and I are doing everything we know to do to instill in them a faith in Jesus Christ . . . but we also recognize that salvation is God's work.

God gives us opportunities. I feel incredibly blessed by the opportunities I have been given. I do my best to seize and build upon each one, but I recognize that only God can bring the opportunities leading to *eternal results*.

God gives us harvest. We each can plant and cultivate, but only God can grow a seed.

I believe very strongly in divine interruptions—times in which God makes Himself and His plan very plain to us. I pray this book would be a divine interruption in your life.

My prayer is also that this book will be a seed sown into your life from which God will grow an amazing harvest. I pray this book will be a God-sent inspiration for you to grow in His Word, and an opportunity for you to make key changes that will result in God's best for your family. I join my mom in praying this book will bless you and your family in ways only God could imagine!

DIVINE INTERRUPTION

*D*ecide today to take a spiritual and pragmatic approach to your family's future by choosing to look at the facts, not with fear, but with faith. See every "red flag" in your family tree as an opportunity for growth and victory. Bear down spiritually through prayer, placing your trust completely in God . . . and your family in His hands.

blessing
the
next generation

1

What's Roosting in Your Family Tree?

Many years ago a woman flew to Mexico to visit missionary friends working on the outskirts of Acapulco. As they left the airport and drove toward the missionary's home, they drove past a tree this woman described to us as "black." She assumed the tree either was an exotic tropical plant with an odd color, or the tree had died and the leaves had turned black but hadn't fallen from the tree—in fact, the leaves still fluttered in the light tropical breeze. The tree gave her a creepy feeling but she quickly turned her attention to other more colorful and interesting sights.

Very early the next morning the woman and her hosts drove past the tree again, and this time, the limbs of the tree were completely bare—there were no leaves in sight, either on the tree or at its base.

"What's with this tree?" the woman asked. "Yesterday it was filled with black leaves, and today it's bare."

"Oh, those weren't leaves," her host explained. "Those were

feathers! That's the vulture tree. The vultures—which are very large, black birds—leave the branches of this dead tree every evening and don't come back until late in the morning. There are so many vultures that when they flock together on this tree, you can hardly see that they are individual birds."

Talk about creepy!

When this woman heard us speak about generational blessings and curses, she relayed this story to us and added, "It sorta makes you wonder, doesn't it, what might be roosting in a person's family tree?"

DOES IT REALLY MATTER?

Does it really matter what is roosting in a person's family tree?

God says it does. From the opening pages of the Bible, God speaks about generations. In the book of Genesis the words *generation* and *generations* are mentioned twenty-one times in the King James Version. In fact, one way to study the Bible is to study it in terms of generations. The passing of faith from generation to generation is a central theme of the Bible.

Even before we have the account of Adam and Eve in the Garden of Eden, we read: "These are the generations of the heavens and of the earth when they were created, in the day that the LORD God made the earth and the heavens" (Gen. 2:4 KJV). Then we read about the descendants of Adam: "This is the book of the generations of Adam" (Gen. 5:1 KJV). In the next chapter we read about Noah: "These are the generations of Noah: Noah was a just man and perfect in his generations, and Noah walked with God" (Gen. 6:9 KJV).

Then the Bible narrows the field of families to focus on the family of Shem: "These are the generations of Shem" (Gen. 11:10 KJV). The name *Shem* means "name"—from Shem would

come the name of all names: Jesus. There would be a line of
people directly from Shem all the way to Jesus. Their identity,
their name, would continue and be enlarged.

As part of that family tree descending from Shem, the
Bible tells us about the "generations of Terah," which included Abraham (Gen. 11:27 KJV). It tells us about the "generations of Ishmael," Abraham's son who was born to Hagar
the Egyptian (Gen. 25:12 KJV), and about the "generations of
Isaac" in whom all of the promises made to Abraham were
confirmed (Gen. 25:19 KJV). The Bible goes on to tell about
the "generations of Esau" and the "generations of Jacob"
(Gen. 36:1, 37:2 KJV).

Why make such a point about the word *generations*? Because throughout the Word of God we find repeated examples
that God desires for families to change, come to completion,
continue, and to experience an increase in blessing. What is
true for Bible families could be very true for *your* family!

THE THREE Cs OF GOD'S PLAN FOR THE GENERATIONS

God's plan is that a family's pattern from generation to generation be this: change, completion, continuation. Let's take a
brief look at each of these Cs:

Change

God wants to change *everything* negative, unproductive, inef-
fective, or sinful into something positive, productive, effective,
and good. (See Romans 8:28.) He wants to change our thinking, our feeling, our believing, and our behavior. He wants to
transform us fully into the character likeness of Jesus Christ.
(See 2 Corinthians 3:18.)

Consider the apostle Paul, a Pharisee who followed the law
precisely but brutally persecuted Christians. God had other

plans for Paul, and through a divine encounter on the road to Damascus, God transformed Paul's heart. From that point on Paul's thoughts, emotions, and actions were conformed to Christ and God used Paul to write two-thirds of the New Testament.

God is always seeking to develop the potential He placed within us, to make us into *all* He initially designed us to be. With His help, we can do *all* we are capable of doing. And since most people only use a small fraction of their brain power and their faith and achieve only a fraction of their potential, there's always room for God to do more in our lives.

God doesn't want you to be barely productive or moderately blessed. God desires a *fullness* that produces an overflow of *abundance*. From the very beginning, God established a principle of multiplication. He commanded Adam and Eve to multiply. He commanded Noah to multiply after the Great Flood. He commands us to multiply. God doesn't do things in a mere additive manner. *He multiplies*. Multiplication produces abundance.

Completion

God wants to heal us where we are weak or diseased—physically, emotionally, mentally, and physically. He wants to fill in the gaps of our lives and make us whole. Repeatedly as Jesus healed people physically, He spoke to them about being made whole.

Jesus healed the man at the pool of Bethesda. He had been ill for thirty-eight years and told Jesus he was unable to get into the pool unassisted. Yet Jesus told him to take up his mat and walk. When Jesus spoke, the man's thinking was changed and he stood up. His body was healed and he walked away—whole. (See John 5:2–9.) That's what God desires for us today. He wants us to be fully functional and at the top of our game.

He wants us to have everything we need to live and to extend the gospel.

Continuation

God wants all the good He establishes in your life to remain or continue. He wants the love and blessings He pours into you to be poured *through you* to others. (See John 15:9.)

An Upward Spiral of Increasing Good. The Bible pattern of change, completion, and continuation is expected to produce *increasing good.* From the very beginning, God commanded Adam and Eve to multiply. Even after they sinned, they were to multiply with the promise that one of their descendants would one day score a definitive victory over sin (Gen. 3:15).

Noah did not continue in the sinful pattern of his ancestors Adam and Eve but was a "just man and perfect" (Gen. 6:9 KJV). He is a superior example that God's forgiveness can be accepted and a family curse of sin can be fully reversed.

God's desire for change, completion, and continuation is that an *upward* spiral be established—one that goes from blessing to greater blessing, good to even greater good, abundance to increased abundance.

FAMILIES *CAN* CHANGE FOR THE BETTER!

Bloodline may be fixed from generation to generation, but a family can change in character and in the way it serves God.

What good news this is! You don't need to continue a negative family pattern. You don't need to pass on traits contrary to God's desire for you or your family.

One of the greatest examples of change in family nature is found in the story of Jacob. Jacob, one of twin boys born to Isaac and Rebekah, was given the name *Jacob* because it means "trickster"—one who tries to lay hold of something that is not his. Jacob was given this name because his hand was grasping the heel of his brother as he came out of Rebekah's womb.

For much of his early life, Jacob exhibited character that was fully in keeping with his name. He tricked his brother, Esau, into giving him the birthright inheritance that should have been Esau's as the firstborn son. He later tricked his father, Isaac, into giving him the blessing that should have been given to Esau. These two acts of deceit forced Jacob into exile. And where did he go? To the home of his uncle Laban, who was a master of deceit.

Laban tricked Jacob into marrying Leah when Jacob thought he was marrying Rachel. Ultimately, Laban tricked Jacob into fourteen years of hard labor. No doubt believing retaliation was fair, Jacob tricked Laban into giving him a large flock of sheep and goats and then left in a deceitful manner, not telling Laban of his plans. (See Genesis 29–31.)

As he made his way back home, Jacob divided his children and servants and flocks into two groups—sending one group with his wife Leah and the other with his wife Rachel while he stayed behind. That night, Jacob had a supernatural "encounter"; he struggled with God's messenger, and God did a most remarkable thing. He changed Jacob's name to *Israel*, which means "contender with God." God's Word tells us that the angel said, "Your name will no longer be Jacob, but Israel, because you have struggled with God and with men and have overcome" (Gen. 32:28 NIV).

In changing Jacob's name, God was changing Jacob's identity—not only the way he saw himself, but the way he presented himself to others, and ultimately, the way his descendants regarded themselves. Jacob did not need to trick his way through life; he could cling to God and trust God to bless him—and in so doing, he would be a prince of God the

Sovereign King. The descendants of Jacob are not known as Jacobites. They are known as *Israelites*. The identity of Jacob became their identity as a people—a people who would be called God's chosen ones.

God never blesses sin. He does forgive and then bless those who seek His forgiveness and who cling to Him. He gives the sinner a new identity—a new name, new character, a new future. If God could change a Jacob, He certainly can change you and me and our children into His likeness.

God's desire is to bless you, to bless your children, and to create a line of generations who both know His blessing and are determined to pass it on. This legacy of blessing is an integral part of the covenant God made with Abraham and his descendants. (See Genesis 12.)

What about you?

Consider your family tree. Is there a point where change was made? Is there something you see that needs changing? Might this change begin with *you*?

Insight from Marilyn

"You have an enlarged heart. There's nothing we can do about it." The physician's words were like a knife thrust deep into my faith. I was only twenty-three years old at the time. I thought immediately, *My father had a heart attack, and now the same thing is going to happen to me!*

If the devil can hold his breath, I feel certain he was holding it in that moment to see how I might respond. I had just recently become Spirit-filled and I knew enough of God's Word to believe Jesus desired me to have an abundant life, and such a life included health. I refused to believe for my father's fate and instead chose to believe in faith for Jesus' healing and health. Later that year I was miraculously healed of having an enlarged heart.

Just a few years ago, I had my annual physical checkup and the physician said to me, "Your heart is excellent!" I knew that to be true in my own spirit and mind, but it was good nonetheless to get a physician's agreement.

When my daughter, Sarah, was a sophomore in college, she called home one evening and said, "Mother, I'm having strange pains in my chest."

The thought came like an echo of the past, *Well, this is it. Sarah has inherited the family trait of an enlarged heart.* But also like an echo, my spirit rose up inside me and I heard myself saying to myself, *Sarah does not have a heart condition. That family curse has not only been broken, but it has been reversed.*

Sarah and I prayed together over the phone and stood in faith against anything the enemy might be trying to do in Sarah's life. The pains left, and Sarah has never had any heart problems.

Let me assure you, whatever it is the devil desires to dredge up from your family past, God desires to heal. What has been cursed, God desires to *reverse* into a blessing. What has been a point of defeat, God desires to turn into a testimony of victory.

What Can Be Passed Down ... and Is

As genome theory has advanced in recent years, we are learning more and more about those things that can and are passed down to us genetically—primarily physical traits, including predisposition to certain ailments, physical weaknesses, or diseases.

We can also be predisposed to *act* in certain ways, both indirectly by the examples of family members' lives and directly by what they taught us verbally. Our parents' and grandparents' behavior, for better or for worse, has been imprinted upon our family tree and will continue to be passed down until something changes.

Insight from Sarah

Years ago my parents encountered a man who had been a burglar as a teenager—and he faced a number of legal problems as a result. He came to faith through my parents' ministry when he was about twenty-one years old, and a few years later, he was filled with God's Spirit and was totally set free from any desire to steal.

One day my mother asked this man about his family. He mentioned a son raised by his ex-wife. Mom asked, "Do you see your son? Is he a Christian?" The man replied, "No, he's in prison."

Mom asked, "What for?" You guessed it. Robbery.

This man had little contact with his son during his son's growing up years, but the devil was able to exploit a generational weakness that had not been dealt with spiritually.

How important it is that we live according to God's commandments and value God's commandments as important. It is equally important to realize generational curses *can be broken.*

ONE OF FOUR . . . OR ONE OF A THOUSAND GENERATIONS?

The Bible tells us family sin can be imprinted on us and can be traced back four generations. (See Exodus 20:5.) God said this to His people as part of His ordinances that we know as the Ten Commandments:

> *Do not make idols of any kind, whether in the shape of birds or animals or fish. You must never worship or bow down to them, for I, the LORD your God, am a jealous God who will not share your affection with any other god!* I do not leave unpunished the sins of those who hate me, but I punish the children for the sins of their parents to the third and fourth generations. But I lavish my love on those who love me and obey my commands, even for a thousand generations. *(Exodus 20:4–6, emphasis added)*

Four or one thousand? God's plan for blessing is far greater than His judgment of sin on this earth. What an encouragement that should be to us!

We need to recognize, however, that sin can leave a deep stain on a family.

Our sin as human beings is directly related to what we worship—to what we give homage, and to what we *serve*. Anything we put as a top priority in our lives is something we *worship*. If we give our time to it more than we give our time to God . . . if we give our talent to it more than we give our talent to God . . . if we give our resources to it more than we make them available to God . . . if we give our interest or thoughts to it more than we give our thoughts and interests to God . . . we are in a state of worshiping something other than God.

And that's not all. What we serve is what we tend to become.

If we serve an addictive substance—giving in to every opportunity that comes our way to take that drug or have that drink—we can become addicts. If we are substance abusers, we will in turn be abused by those substances. If we obey and serve Almighty God, we become more and more like God in our character and in our behavior. (See 2 Corinthians 3:18.) If we worship someone other than God, we become more like that entity or person. Just look at all the young people today who want to become like the celebrities they idolize.

If we serve the lusts of our flesh, we reap lust-related sins.

If we serve our inner greed, we reap material-related sins.

If we serve our inner desire for power or fame, we reap relational sins.

The sins we willfully pursue can be imprinted on our lives and on our children, grandchildren, and great-grandchildren, and even our great-great-grandchildren.

The evidence is all around us. Those who worship at the altar of sexual promiscuity and "free love" are anything but free—they are subject to all sorts of sex-related diseases and broken relationships. Those who worship at the altar of making money are anything but rich emotionally and spiritually—they are subject to all sorts of stress, anxiety, and fears related to today's fluctuating markets. Those who worship the positions they have achieved are always disappointed—there's always someone who comes along to snatch the limelight or the top rung of the ladder.

What we worship eventually comes to light, just as seedlings sprout from hidden seeds and eventually grow and produce fruit. The fruit of our sin may take years to become visible. Indeed, it may take decades—the fruit may not be fully visible until the next generation.

What a warning this should be to those who say, "It's my own private sin. It's nobody's business what I do behind closed doors." In truth, there are no "private" sins. All sin has consequences in your life, in the lives of those around you, or in the lives of your unborn heirs.

Part of the description the Lord gave of Himself to Moses included these words:

> I am the LORD, I am the LORD, the merciful and gracious God. I am slow to anger and rich in unfailing love and faithfulness. I show this unfailing love to many thousands by forgiving every kind of sin and rebellion. Even so I do not leave sin unpunished, but I punish the children for the sins of their parents to the third and fourth generations. (Exodus 34:6–7)

Here, in a few brief lines, is a picture of God's balanced justice. On the one hand, we have God's mercy, patience, and an abundance of goodness, truth, mercy, and forgiveness. On the other hand, God allows the iniquity of a person to be visited upon that person's heirs. The sins of the fathers are passed down because they have not been cleared.

This is a vitally important concept for you to understand. The way we are set free from the iniquity of the fathers is God's merciful and generous *forgiveness.*

That is the powerful promise of the New Testament!

We do not need to be trapped by the sins of those who have gone before us. We do not need to live out the predisposition for ungodly behavior placed within us. We can make a choice to seek God's forgiveness, and in so doing, we can reverse the curse of what has been planted in us.

The opportunity to seek God's forgiveness is given to every person. No person is denied this choice. Even those who do not grow up in a Christian environment have a basic understanding of God and of the void in their lives only God can fill. When a person seeks, he finds. When he asks, God answers.

The sin nature with us from birth can be cleansed. The curse of generational sin can be reversed.

Insight from Marilyn

Earlier, Sarah mentioned to you a man who told me about his son's being in prison. I encouraged this man to go to his son. I explained to him the power of forgiveness in breaking the bond of generational sin. I said, "The evil spirit who tempted you to be a thief has no hold on your life, but it does have hold on your son's life. You must go to your son. He is eighteen years old, so he has to make a decision himself. You, as his father, can pray powerfully that the enemy of deception will be revealed. You can and must go to your son and say to him, 'Son, I got into burglary when I was your age, and this is why I did it. The devil influenced me to steal, and what the devil encourages a person to do to others, he also does to us. The devil stole from my life. I thought I was stealing from others, but the devil was actually stealing from me. I was the one who was getting robbed the most. One of the things I was robbed of was a relationship with you. I know that, and I'm sorry for that. Now this evil spirit has come against you because you are my son. Satan knows this weakness was planted in you. Evil spirits have prompted you and tempted you to do what you have done. If you want to be free of this influence in your life, however, you can be free just as I was made free. You can choose to trust in Jesus as your Savior and you can choose to follow Jesus as your Lord.'"

And then, I told this father that he must pray.

"But what if my son doesn't want me to pray?" the man asked.

I said, "If your son is ready to make a decision about Jesus, you can lead him in a prayer, but if he says, 'I'm not ready,' then you can tell him, 'Someday, son, you may be ready so I want to tell you how to pray when that day comes.' Then, pray a simple prayer he can remember."

"What would you pray?" he asked.

I said, "I'd pray, 'Father, forgive me in particular for robbery and burglary. Satan has tempted me in this way and it's come against my life and deceived me. I am deeply sorry I listened to the devil's voice. I know I have done wrong and I ask You to forgive me and to put me in right relationship with You. I ask You to help me to live free of the devil's influence on my life from this day forward. I ask this on the basis of what Jesus did for me on the Cross. I believe Jesus died for my sins so I could come to this moment and be set free of them.'"

"Is there anything else I should do?" the man asked.

"Yes," I said. "Assure your son that when he asks for God's forgiveness, God will forgive—instantly and completely. The Bible says, 'If we confess our sins to him, he is faithful and just to forgive us and to cleanse us from every wrong (1 John 1:9).' You might want to memorize that verse before you go to visit your son, or write it down and take it on a small card you can leave with your son. Assure your son that while he may have been a thief in the past, he never needs to be a thief again. There is a cleansing that breaks the pattern of generational sin. Your son can put an axe to the root of this sin, chopping it down so it cannot continue to grow or bear bad fruit in his life."

WHAT CANNOT BE PASSED DOWN

One thing that cannot be passed down from one generation to the next is perhaps the most important thing of all: a personal relationship with Jesus Christ. God doesn't have any grandchildren. Every person is required to accept Jesus as Savior, as an act of his own will and faith. Every person must choose to follow Jesus as Lord, again as an act of his own will and faith.

Certainly all Christian parents want to see their children choose Jesus as Savior and Lord. Even more than we desire this, God desires this. He *wants* our children and grandchildren to be in intimate relationship with Him and to serve Him all the days of their lives.

The enemy of our souls, however—whom Jesus called the *thief and robber, the father of all lies,* and *the devil*—desires to stop God's truth from operating beyond your own life and generation.

One of the devil's methods for discouraging your children and grandchildren from accepting and following Jesus is to exploit any family weakness—physical, moral, and emotional—and to use it to tempt your children to sin and reject the truth. Nothing hurts or discourages a parent more than to have a child who rejects the Lord. What we need to recognize is that the devil knows how much we suffer when our children reject Jesus Christ. We need to recognize that the devil purposefully targets our children, in part to get to *us* as parents and grandparents.

YOUR CHILDREN ARE BEING TARGETED

No person can ever mature spiritually to the point the devil is prevented from tempting that person. When a demon is denied entrance into a person's life—because of that person's faith in

Jesus as Savior or because of his ongoing commitment to obey God—the demon has no opportunity for direct influence.

However, the devil will seek to indwell and influence someone who is *close* to the one who has denied him power or control. Typically that close person is another family member—a spouse, a child, a grandchild, perhaps a brother or sister.

Do you know someone so preoccupied with a spouse's sin he or she has stopped doing what God called that person to do—or a parent who has become so filled with hurt and concern he has begun to distrust God?

The Bible tells us the devil's secondary efforts are seven times more wicked! Read what Jesus taught:

> *When an evil spirit leaves a person, it goes into the desert, seeking rest but finding none. Then it says, "I will return to the person I came from." So it returns and finds its former home empty, swept, and clean. Then the spirit finds seven other spirits more evil than itself, and they all enter the person and live there. And so that person is worse off than before. (Matthew 12:43–45)*

If you are a Christian parent today, take note. The devil will come after those you love with even more potent temptations than you ever experienced—in fact, seven times more potent.

The Bible also speaks of some demons as being "familiar spirits." Demons are familiar with history. They know your family tree, perhaps better than you do. They know the weaknesses and sinful behaviors lurking in your family history, and they know how to exploit these past patterns and behaviors in a way that attacks or tempts your children. They know the generational curses that have come upon your family.

WHAT EXACTLY IS A GENERATIONAL CURSE?

A generational curse is an iniquity that increases in strength from one generation to the next, affecting the members of a family and all who come into relationship with that family.

How can you tell if you are under the influence of a generational curse? Here's a simple test. Consider not only yourself but your entire family—previous generations, the current generation, and the future generation—as you answer yes or no to the following questions:

1. Do you recognize a pattern of failure?
2. Is there a history of premature death or suicide in your family?
3. Do you exhibit a high level of anger?
4. Have you experienced a high incidence of accidents, or accidents that are unusual in nature?
5. Is there a history of abuse—physical, emotional, or sexual?
6. Is there a history of chronic illness, including long-term health problems and repeated colds and bouts of flu?
7. Is there a history of mental illness that seems to have progressed through the generations?
8. Are any of these personality behaviors prevalent: control, manipulation, addiction, codependency, depression, unforgiveness, or social isolation?

A yes answer to any of these questions could be a symptom of a generational curse.

Generational Blessings

What is a generational blessing? It is the opposite of generational curse. Here is a very simple but accurate definition:

*To flow in the current of generational blessings means
to experience a consistent and ongoing stream of
all that is good, beneficial, and positive
from God's perspective.*

Generational blessing is the establishment of God's best—physically, emotionally, relationally, and spiritually. It is the creation of a heritage of goodness and wholeness.

IS YOUR FAMILY MORE LIKE THE EDWARDS, OR THE JUKES?

One of the most profound examples we have ever read of families exhibiting blessing or curse is the example of the Edwards and Jukes families.

Jonathan Edwards and Max Jukes were contemporaries. Their lives, however, could not have been more different. Edwards was a committed Christian minister who gave God first place in his life and married a godly woman. Jukes was an atheist who married a godless woman.

A man once studied the descendants of these two men over a period of time. This is what he found:

Of the 540 descendants of Max Jukes who could be traced, 310 died as paupers. One hundred and fifty became criminals, including seven murderers. One hundred were known to be drunkards, and at least half of the women were prostitutes. The antics of Max Jukes's descendants cost the United States government more than $1.25 million.

Of the 1,394 descendants that could be traced to Jonathan Edwards, 295 graduated from college, thirteen became college presidents, and sixty-five became professors. Three were elected to be United States senators, and another eighty held some form of public office. One served as vice president of the United States.

Thirty were judges, one hundred were lawyers. Sixty were physicians, and seventy-five became officers in the military.

One hundred were missionaries and preachers; sixty were prominent authors. None of Edwards's descendants was a liability to the government.

A lineage of blessing, or of cursing?

Consider your own family tree. Are you trusting God to establish or continue a lineage of blessing, or are you expecting the curse to run its course in your family?

There's good news—a lineage of generational curses can be turned around—and the change can begin *now*. It only takes one person in a family to turn things around. That one can be you!

DIVINE INTERRUPTION

To flow in the current of generational blessing means to experience, throughout your family tree, a consistent and ongoing stream of all that is good, beneficial, and positive from God's perspective. Prayerfully assess your family's past and present; then choose to be a catalyst for change.

2

Turn It Around!

M ost people don't know very much about a young woman named Jehosheba. She was the bride of a young priest, and she is one of the unsung heroines of the Bible.

Jehosheba had possibly the worst family tree of anyone in the Bible, with the possible exception of the Herod family in New Testament times. She lived in ancient Israel and the book of Kings tells her family story.

Jehosheba's great-grandfather was Omri, an ungodly king of the northern kingdom called Israel. Omri was a shrewd politician who sought to make peace with the neighboring nation of Zidon by arranging for his son Ahab to marry a woman named Jezebel. Few women were ever as wicked as Queen Jezebel, who introduced the nation of Israel to the worship of Baal—the most demonic religion of that day.

The prophet Elijah opposed Ahab and Jezebel and pronounced God's punishment of a drought upon the land. After three years of drought, Elijah challenged the prophets of Baal to a showdown on Mount Carmel. All day, the prophets of Baal sought to have their sacrifice accepted by their gods. Meanwhile, Elijah prepared an altar, dug a moat around it, and filled the moat with water as he drenched the sacrifice he placed upon the altar.

At the time of the evening sacrifice, Elijah asked the Lord to honor his sacrifice. Immediately the Lord sent fire from heaven to consume the sacrifice, the altar, the dirt around the base of the altar, and all the water. Elijah slew the four hundred prophets of Baal and then he called upon the Lord to end the drought. His prayer was answered even before Elijah and King Ahab could get back to the city of Jezreel. Elijah also prophesied a curse upon Ahab and Jezebel and their descendants for leading Israel into evil.

Meanwhile, many miles south, King Jehoshaphat, a righteous king of the southern kingdom called Judah, arranged an alliance he hoped would bring peace between the northern and southern kingdoms. Jehoshaphat accepted a marriage between his son, Jehoram, and Athalia, the daughter of Jezebel. Instead of Jehoram's influencing Athalia for good, Athalia corrupted Jehoram and all of Judah by introducing the worship of her mother's religion, Baal, to Judah.

Oh, how many times *that* happens—we think we are going to influence people for good, only to discover they have a far greater influence on us for bad.

Eight years after Jehoram became king of Judah, he died in battle. The son of Jehoram and Athalia—Ahaziah—became king. He ruled for only one year and was also killed. One of Ahaziah's sons should have become king, according to the laws of succession. However, Athalia saw her son's death as a golden opportunity to seize control of the throne of Judah. To ensure the success of her plan, she sent assassins to murder all of her grandsons.

It is hard to imagine a woman so evil she would seek the deaths of all her grandsons so she might rule with unchallenged power. More than the throne was at stake and the devil knew it. God said the Messiah would come through the seed of David, and had Athaliah succeeded in killing *all* her male grandchildren, the Davidic line would have ended at that point.

This is where Jehosheba enters the story. Jehosheba was the daughter of Athaliah and Jehoram. When Jehosheba heard what her mother was plotting, she slipped into the nursery and saved the youngest grandson from the assassin's blade. She and her husband secretly guarded the child, whose name was Joash, until he was seven years old. On Joash's seventh birthday, he was brought to the temple and crowned king. The nation rallied around young Joash and Athalia was killed. Jehosheba reintroduced blessing into a family tree that had become horribly corrupt.

No matter how much evil, dysfunction, disease, or emotional sickness may exist in your family's background, don't despair. God can and will turn around those conditions as you choose to do what is right in His eyes. One person *can* make an eternal difference.

BELIEVING FOR YOUR FAMILY

The Bible has an amazing story about the apostle Paul and his traveling companion Silas. They were arrested after casting out a demon from a young slave woman who was controlled by a spirit of divination. The young woman's owners had gained a great deal of money from her soothsaying and they were very angry at Paul and Silas for ending her career. They insisted the magistrates of the city whip Paul and Silas severely and then throw them into prison.

While in prison, Paul and Silas began to pray and sing praises to God—loud enough to conduct an evangelistic rally right there among the prisoners. Suddenly a great earthquake shook the foundation of the prison, the doors flew open, and the bands on the prisoners were loosed.

The keeper of the prison awoke. Seeing the prison doors open, he became filled with terror. The prisoners were his responsibility; if they escaped, his own life was in jeopardy. He was about to kill himself when Paul cried out, "Don't do it! We are all here!"

> *Trembling with fear, the jailer called for lights and ran to the dungeon and fell down before Paul and Silas. He brought them out and asked, "Sirs, what must I do to be saved?"*
>
> *They replied, "Believe on the Lord Jesus and you will be saved, along with* your *entire household." (Acts 16:28–31, emphasis added)*

Paul and Silas then shared the gospel with everybody in the prison keeper's household. They all received Jesus as their Savior. That very night, the prison keeper and his family washed the wounds of Paul and Silas. The disciples, in turn, baptized his entire household. The newly converted family and Paul and Silas shared a wonderful meal together and rejoiced because the prison keeper "and *his entire household* . . . believed in God" (Acts 16:34, emphasis added).

God's desire is for your entire family to know the joy of salvation as they follow Jesus and spread the good news for the rest of their days.

Insight from Marilyn

Before I was saved and filled with God's Spirit, I attended a Sunday school class. One day I challenged everything the teacher said. It's rather embarrassing now to recall some of the ridiculous statements I made. It was obvious I didn't believe in Jesus—and I didn't care who knew it.

You can imagine how concerned I was when my daughter went to Germany for a summer while she was in college, and upon her return to the United States, she told me she didn't believe in Jesus. My heart sank to my feet as I listened to her say some of the very things I said so long ago in that Sunday school class. It was as if my words were echoing through the decades—she was speaking the same phrases and sentences I once spoke.

I knew my daughter was raised in a Spirit-filled home, brought up on the Word of God, and received the Lord at an early age. She was a student at Oral Roberts University. All of these facts made her words more difficult to hear. The Lord, however, spoke deep in my spirit and said, "Don't fall apart—be cool!" So I told my daughter, "Sarah, we loved you before you were born, and you didn't know Jesus then. We love you now and always will. You will come out of this with stronger faith than ever before." Needless to say, my husband, Wally, and I began to pray unceasingly.

If your child is rebelling against God today, my foremost word to you is this: pray, and don't stop praying. Pray with faith, because God can reach your child in ways you cannot.

It is equally important to let your child see that your love is unconditional. Keep the lines of communication open. When Sarah was estranged from the Lord, the last thing she needed was to be estranged from her parents. Don't judge or condemn a rebellious child—instead, speak words of life, love, and faith.

It wasn't long before Sarah called us to tell us she had recommitted her life to Christ. And the words I spoke in that earlier fearful moment came to pass: *her faith grew stronger than ever.*

God is faithful! The enemy may try to discourage you by playing a reprise of your unredeemed past in your children's lives. Though your heart may quake, stand firm, trusting God to protect your child. Don't quit praying, no matter what your child says or does. Don't quit believing God can and will be victorious in your child's life.

YOUR DESCENDANTS AND YOUR "UP-LINE"

We tend to think in terms of generational blessing being only for our descendants. It is also for those who are in our "up-line"—our parents and grandparents who are still alive. We can be instrumental in sharing the Word of God and the plan of salvation with them.

Years ago, a man we'll call Bill worked at Marilyn Hickey Ministries. He told us the story of his family.

After Bill came to know the Lord, he immediately began to pray that his parents would also come to know the Lord. That is the first reaction of most people when they are born again. They want to share their salvation with all their relatives—they want their *earthly* family to be included in their *heavenly* family.

Bill's parents were in their seventies, so he quickly arranged for a visit home to tell his parents about what happened to him spiritually. He felt led by the Holy Spirit to ask his mother, "Mom, have you ever really received the Lord into your heart?" She said, "No, I never have, not in the way you are describing." She had a tender heart and was open to the things Bill shared with her. She prayed with Bill to receive Jesus as her Savior and began to read her Bible and grow in her faith as the days passed after his visit.

Bill's father, however, had a very different reaction. He was the kind of person who argued, "I have never smoked. I don't drink. I don't curse. I've taken good care of my family, given to charity, and been 'good' all my life." He figured that was enough to merit salvation and he was offended at any suggestion that he might need to do something else to qualify for heaven.

Bill asked the Lord, "What about my dad? What can I say that will get through to him?" Bill cried out for God's wisdom to know the right words and the right timing.

During a family reunion, Bill felt led of the Holy Spirit to have a private conversation with his father. He said, "Dad, you know I don't want to offend you. I don't want to hurt your feelings. But I am concerned about you. I love you. I just want to share Jesus with you one more time, because I don't believe you can make it to heaven solely on the good things you have done—no matter how good they've been. I think you're going to miss it, Dad, and I don't want that to happen."

To Bill's surprise, his father started weeping and he confessed, "You know, son, I think I'm going to miss it, too." Bill was able to lead his father to the Lord that afternoon. The entire family enjoyed warm fellowship in God for all the remaining years that Bill's parents were alive, and when they died, Bill had full assurance his parents were in heaven.

The Bible has numerous examples of entire families who came to know the Lord and serve the Lord.

Noah and His Entire Family Were Saved in the Ark.
When God saw the world awash in depravity and sin, He also saw a righteous man and spoke to him. The Bible tells us: "The LORD then said to Noah, 'Go into the ark, *you and your whole family*, because I have found you righteous in this generation.' . . . And Noah and his sons and his wife and his sons' wives entered the ark to escape the waters of the flood" (Gen. 7:1,7 NIV, emphasis added).

God Made a Covenant with Abraham and Promised Its Continuation Throughout Abraham's Generations.
As a symbol of God's covenant with Abraham, the patriarch and his male descendants would be circumcised. The covenant was for all who would descend from Abraham, both physically and spiritually. The Bible records God's words:

> *I will continue this everlasting covenant between us, generation after generation. It will continue between me and your offspring forever. And I will always be your God and the God of your descendants after you. Yes, I will give all this land of Canaan to you and to your offspring forever. And I will be their God.*
> *. . . This is the covenant that you and your descendants must keep: Each male among you must be circumcised. . . . This applies not only to members of your family, but also to the servants born in your household and the foreign-born servants whom you have purchased. . . . Your bodies will thus bear the mark of my everlasting covenant. (Genesis 17:7–8,10,12–13)*

In Jericho, God Spared Rahab's Entire Family.
Rahab, a harlot, provided shelter for two spies sent into Jericho by Joshua to scope out the city and its defense system.

In return for her kindness, Rahab and her family were given safe passage out of the city when the day of destruction came. Joshua's instructions were clear: "The city and everything in it must be completely destroyed as an offering to the LORD. Only *Rahab the prostitute and the others in her house* will be spared, for she protected our spies" (Josh. 6:17, emphasis added).

Jesus Brought Salvation to Zaccheus's Family.
When Jesus encountered Zaccheus, the man had climbed up a tree in order to get a better view of Jesus as He passed through the city. Recognizing the man's faith, Jesus invited Himself to a meal at Zacchaeus's house. The Bible tells us:

> *When Jesus came by, he looked up at Zacchaeus and called him by name. "Zacchaeus!" he said. "Quick, come down! For I must be a guest in your home today." . . . "Salvation has come to* this home *today, for this man has shown himself to be a son of Abraham. And I, the Son of Man, have come to seek and save those like him who are lost"* (Luke 19:5, 9–10, emphasis added).

When Jesus Healed a Nobleman's Son, the Entire Household Was Impacted.
The Bible says:

> *There was a government official in the city of Capernaum whose son was very sick. When he heard that Jesus had come from Judea and was traveling in Galilee, he went over to Cana. He found Jesus and begged him to come to Capernaum with him to heal his son, who was about to die.*

Jesus asked, "Must I do miraculous signs and won-ders before you people will believe in me?"

The official pleaded, "Lord, please come now before my little boy dies."

Then Jesus told him, "Go back home. Your son will live!" And the man believed Jesus' word and started home.

While he was on his way, some of his servants met him with the news that his son was alive and well. He asked them when the boy had begun to feel better, and they replied, "Yesterday afternoon at one o'clock his fever suddenly disappeared!" Then the father realized it was the same time that Jesus had told him, "Your son will live." And the officer and his entire household believed in Jesus (John 4:46–53, emphasis added).

Are you starting to see the big picture of God's plan? God desires to bless entire families—and to bless the world through them.

Insight from Marilyn

My mother was from a very large family—she was one of eleven children—and when she became Spirit-filled, her fam-ily cut her off. They wanted nothing to do with her. But when my mother's sister Juanita became born again and Spirit-filled, she and my mother prayed faithfully for the whole family.

Both Mother and Juanita are in heaven now, but by the time Mother died, all but one of her family members had ac-cepted Jesus as Savior. And, several of my mother's nieces and nephews have become involved in full-time ministry.

Recently at a partner breakfast a woman named Carrie

approached me and said, "I am related to you." When she mentioned her dad's name, I realized her father was Juanita's son, Kent, who was my favorite cousin. Carrie explained that she had been privileged to lead her father to Christ.

I was so overjoyed I could have cried a bucket of tears. How I wished I could telephone my mother in heaven so we could rejoice together . . . but we will *someday*!

✒

Insight from Sarah

We have a friend named John who is a pastor in Australia. John's father came from a long line of alcoholics—alcohol abuse was a generational curse in their family.

Then John's father gave his life to Christ through the ministry of the Salvation Army. He made a decision that the alcoholism in their family would stop with him. He became a pastor and he and John's mother had seven children. One of the seven has died, but the remaining children are all involved in ministry. Now, more than half of the grandchildren are serving God, are working in the ministry, or are pastors' wives. What an amazing example of a generational curse that has been turned into a blessing and passed on to two generations—and all from just one man's decision and faith in Christ.

DON'T WITHHOLD THE BEST NEWS!

The word *gospel* means "good news." The very best news of all time is that Jesus died on a cross, shedding His blood as a sacrificial offering for *our* sin, so that we might be forgiven of our sin nature and come into an intimate relationship with God, our heavenly Father. There's no greater hope than this!

Be the one to share the plan of salvation with your children and grandchildren. Be the one to tell your grandchildren the good news that they can be forgiven of their sins and live forever in a one-on-one relationship with God!

Don't Withhold the Truth about the Consequences of Sin, Either.

Just as you want to bless your children with the good news, you want to protect your children by sharing the truth about sin—not to *scare* your children, but to arm them with understanding. Of course, you will want to wait until your children understand the difference between right and wrong and realize that behavior has consequences. When that time comes, be frank and straightforward; your children will appreciate your candor.

You may need to admit to your children that you made mistakes in the past. It's not wrong to say to them, "I blew it when I was your age and I learned some things the hard way. I had a weakness in this area, but I have repented and God has cleansed me. I do not want to see this tendency produce terrible consequences in your life."

A friend of ours is very sensitive to cigarette smoke. He can tell if someone has been smoking even when others can't. One day his thirteen-year-old son came through the front door and he quickly determined that his son had been smoking.

When his father asked him who had given him the cigarette, the boy at first denied smoking. The father shared, "I don't want you to compound what has already happened by lying to get around it. Let me tell you a story." He invited his son to sit on the front porch. There they crunched on apples and talked man-to-man. The father told his son how he tried smoking when he was a teen—and he admitted to his son he quickly became addicted. Since the father had little money as a young teenager, he started stealing from his parents in order to buy cigarettes, and one day, he stole a pack from a neighborhood grocery store. He got caught—not only smoking, but lying about it and stealing to support the habit. "And it wasn't even illegal in those days for a young boy to have cigarette. Now it is, you know," the father said.

"Yeah, I know," the boy agreed.

"I was really upset with myself," the father said. "Not that I had been caught red-handed, but that I hadn't had the courage to say no to the two guys who encouraged me to start smoking. I didn't have the guts to say to them, 'Hey, I don't want anything to do with that habit.' It's hard to say no to friends who try to get you to do something you know is wrong, but when you really think about it, a person who tries to get you to smoke really isn't that good a friend."

The boy nodded silently.

The father continued, "Do you know the worst part?"

The son shook his head.

"The worst part was that I was already addicted by the time I got caught. I had only been smoking regularly for a few months, but I was hooked. I had a terrible time giving up nicotine. Even when I made a decision to give up smoking, and even after I prayed to give up those cigarettes, I struggled to break free from the habit. God helped me and I haven't smoked a cigarette since I was thirteen—but it was hard, son. It was *really* hard."

"Are you saying I'm addicted to nicotine?" the boy asked.

"I don't know if you are," the father said. "But I know the younger you are when you start smoking, the easier it is to become addicted. Not only that, but there's a much greater likelihood you'll have serious health problems—not just later in life, but in high school. Smoking can really hurt your athletic performance. You're a good athlete, son, but even if you decide not to try out for a team, you'll want to have as much energy as possible to enjoy your life and have fun with your friends, right?"

The boy nodded.

The father offered to pray with him to ask God's help in giving up cigarettes, and the boy not only allowed his dad to pray but also joined in the prayer and asked God to forgive him for lying and for not having the fortitude to say no to the friend who offered him the cigarettes.

The father gave his son a big hug as they went back into the house. "I love you, son," he said. "I don't want to see anything keep you from enjoying life and experiencing all God has for you."

This father did so many things right.

He confronted his son. He was vulnerable in sharing his own story. He used reason and facts. He voiced his concern for his son's future. He expressed his love. He prayed with his son. And he didn't soft-pedal the truth that behavior has consequences.

Tell Your Children about the "New Nature" and How to Receive It.

While it is important to tell the whole truth, be careful not to overwhelm your children with an awareness of sin. Share with your children the promise of the new nature. Explain the Bible's assurance that "those who become Christians become new persons. They are not the same anymore, for the old life is gone. A new life has begun!" (2 Cor. 5:17). Also share the fact that believers can be victorious over sin because "the power of the life-giving Spirit has freed [us] through Christ Jesus from the power of sin that leads to death" (Rom. 8:2).

Inspire your children to walk with God. Help them understand that those who receive Christ Jesus are no longer victims of their own weakness or their family's weakness—they are victorious members of the family of God.

Your Children Must Make Decisions of Their Own.
Finally, and very importantly, make sure your children understand fully that they are responsible for making their own personal choices when it comes to accepting Jesus as Savior and following Jesus as Lord.

If you have never made a personal decision for Christ in *your* life, now is the perfect time.

Insight from Sarah

I am so grateful for all my parents have taught me and for the ways in which they so carefully nurtured me. I also appreciate the free will God gives each of us.

It is clear to me from my own spiritual journey that children do not necessarily come to faith exactly as their parents did. My mom and dad made their decisions about Jesus Christ in different ways from me.

During the time my mom mentioned earlier, when I decided against faith in Jesus, I was on a personal journey, searching for the belief system that felt right for *me*. I wasn't sorry I was the daughter of Marilyn and Wally Hickey, but I wanted and needed to be my own person, able to make my own decisions. I believe every young person feels that way at some point.

I studied Hinduism, Buddhism, and Islam. I was very serious about my quest and took a very logical, cerebral approach to my research. As I look back, I realize that although I thought I was heading in a direction all my own, the Holy Spirit was actually guiding my study. I began to think, *If there* is *a God who wants a relationship with me, He* would *capital-ize on human selfishness by offering His Son as a sacrifice in my place. That would reach me!*

Around that time, I believe the Holy Spirit led me to read *Mere Christianity*, a book by C. S. Lewis. Perhaps more than any other factor, the methodical presentation of that book brought me to the moment when I was ready to say, "God, I don't have much faith in You, but what I do have, I give to You." God picked me up right where I was and began to lead me into deeper and deeper faith.

My decision for Jesus Christ was not any less real or lasting because I came to faith this way. If anything, I think it gave me a greater appreciation for the painstaking journey to faith many young people take.

As I think about it, God reached out to me in so many supernatural ways. One thing Mom didn't tell you was that I had a friend at ORU, Mike, with whom I could discuss various ideas and decisions. Mike studied at Harvard before he came to ORU and he was very smart. He was a language major, as I was, and I found him easy to relate to. He had already made a solid faith decision for Christ, and what he had to say chal-lenged me and encouraged me at the same time.

Amazingly, there was also a generation blessing involved in all of this. Years before, Mike's father had been saved and filled with the Spirit under my parents' ministry. Now, when I needed it most, Mike was there.

Insight from Marilyn

Let me add a little something here.

When Sarah first went to Oral Roberts University, I was

like most mothers who send a child off to college. I was concerned about whom she would meet and what ideas she might encounter. I knew a number of the professors at ORU and I trusted them to teach the truth in the classroom, but I certainly didn't know all the students or their families. As I was praying about this one day, the Lord spoke to my heart, saying He was in charge of Sarah's life and that I needed to trust Him to do things His way in her life, in His timing, and using His methods and means.

When Sarah told me about her friendship with Mike, I could see God's hand at work behind the scenes. Here was a young man whose father had been influenced by our ministry, who had been taught the principles of God by godly parents, and who was now in a position to influence my daughter for the Lord. Isn't God amazing? When you help others in His name, watch how God will send help to your own family!

Insight from Sarah

As you pray for your children to accept Jesus Christ, pray God will lead your children to develop friendships with the children of godly parents. Pray that, when they get a little older, they will develop friendships with Christian peers. Pray that your children will have a support group of peers who can help them walk with Christ.

My husband and I pray often that our children will be attracted to friends who love Jesus more than anything else. We know what a difference the right friends will make in their lives.

A Decision to Follow Jesus as Lord.

As your children make decisions for Christ, help them understand the importance of developing a deeper relationship with Christ day by day. Reversing generational curses begins with accepting Jesus Christ as Savior; however, that is not the final step in overcoming the iniquity that may be roosting in your family tree. We turn there next.

POWER POINT

You can be your child's first and foremost evangelist by being the one to share the plan of salvation. You can also reach back to the generations behind you—your parents and grandparents—to share the good news. God will show you which words to say and will prompt you when the timing is just right.

3

Confront Your Daddy's Demons

"My father was a scoundrel," a woman once said to us. "I think he had demons."

As we continued to listen to her tell about a very abusive and ugly childhood, she said through her tears, "Do you think my daddy's demons are still in our family tree?"

Our response? "If they are, let's cast them out!" We had a powerful time of prayer with this woman and she told us she had a new feeling of freedom in her own heart.

Today is the day to confront whatever evil you believe may be lingering in your heritage. That includes confronting the three types of sin described in the Bible—and confronting each of them head-on.

"Sin is sin," you might be saying.

Well, yes . . . and no. The Bible uses very specific words, in very specific ways, to explain God's plan and desire for us.

Isn't it wonderful that we can *know* God's plan and purposes? The Word of God reveals many of the processes God has set into place. We can know His guidelines, His principles, and the goals He has for each of us—both individually and as the body of Christ.

Not long ago, after hearing us speak about generational curses and blessings, a woman asked, "Do I really have to understand how all this works? I just want to do what I have to do to be free of the curse and into the blessing."

No, you really don't need to know all the details about how God works to transform curses into blessing from one generation to the next. But if you are truly going to get to the root of what is wrong, or if you want to be used by God to help another person overcome generational curses, you will *want* to understand what your role is.

It's a little like operating a car. Most of us don't want to know how the transmission on a car works—we just want to get in the car, turn on the ignition, and drive. But if your car has transmission problems, it helps to be able to recognize when something is wrong. And if you want to be a good auto mechanic, you need to know how to fix a transmission problem. The same principle applies here. Unless we understand the basic ideas related to sin and how to overcome it, we can't fully grasp all that is involved in turning a generational curse into a generational blessing.

THE BASICS OF GOD'S THREE-STEP PROCESS

Turning generational sin into generational blessing is essentially a three-step process.

Step 1: Recognize *sin and generational curses.*
Step 2: Turn *from sin and generational curses and* turn toward *salvation and generational blessing.*

Step 3: Decide *you will initiate a heritage of blessing, even if you are the only one.*

There are three terms or phrases that deserve our attention here: *righteousness, Savior and Lord,* and *sanctification.*

Righteousness

The first word that is key to our understanding of generational blessings is *righteousness.*

In today's world, few people seem to want to be known as righteous.

Well . . . do *you?*

The word *righteous* is unfamiliar in our secular culture, but it is of extraordinary importance. To be righteous simply means that a person is in right standing with God. When your relationship is right with God, then everything else can become right. A person whose relationship with God is sound can develop healthy attitudes and beliefs, as well as right behavior.

Righteousness is an important concept to understand as we confront generational curses and seek to turn them into generational blessings. Righteousness is the goal. It is the very essence of experiencing a generational blessing. It is the key to having the *best* God has for us in every area of life.

Savior and Lord

A second important concept is expressed in a phrase used by believers to describe Jesus Christ: *Savior and Lord.*

When we accept Jesus as our Savior, we are acknowledging with our will and our faith that Jesus' death on the cross—the only sacrifice necessary for us to be forgiven of sin—was for us *personally.* All God requires of us is to *believe* in what Jesus did, *believe* He is the Son of God, and *receive* Him as the one who saves us from eternal death and gives us eternal life.

This is the heart of the born-again experience, the way in which we receive a new spirit and a new nature. The *real person* deep inside us is changed the instant we accept Jesus Christ as our Savior. We are forgiven completely and we are given everlasting life (John 3:16). The Holy Spirit becomes available to us as never before and we become *fully able* to live a godly life. The slate is clean—we are in right standing with God, and therefore, in position to establish right things in our lives.

We then must make a decision with our will and by faith to follow and obey Jesus as our *Lord*. We are empowered to do this because Jesus sends the Holy Spirit to help us to live righteously.

Many Christians are surprised as they continue to follow Jesus as their Lord to discover they still give in to temptation from time to time. They do things they don't really *want* to do. They submit to experiences they don't really *want* to have—they just don't know what to do about them. Many of these tendencies are the result of generational curses, patterns set in motion in our families, often before we were born.

Following Jesus as *Lord* means a person is seeking to be in right relationship with God *and* to live a "right life." The ongoing process that produces right living is one of continual cleansing, renewal, and spiritual growth.

Sanctification

The Bible word for the process of ongoing cleansing, renewal, and growth is *sanctification.*

Christianity has its five-dollar words, doesn't it?

Sanctification simply means "to set apart"—to set aside anything that isn't right in God's eyes, and therefore, to be in position to be used fully for God's purposes.

"But what," you may be saying, "does this have to do with generational blessings and curses?"

A great deal! Sanctification brings the soul of man—the mind, will, and emotions—into alignment with the reborn spirit. Until the *soul* matures in this way, the door is left open to generational curses. The apostle Paul wrote about this:

> *And may the God of peace Himself* sanctify you
> through and through [separate you from profane
> things, make you pure and wholly consecrated to God];
> *and may your spirit and soul and body be preserved
> sound* and *complete [and found] blameless at the com-
> ing of our Lord Jesus Christ. (1 Thessalonians 5:23 AMP,
> emphasis added)*

Paul also explained sanctification from a slightly different perspective: "Therefore, my beloved, as you have always obeyed, not as in my presence only, but now much more in my absence, work out your own salvation with fear and trembling; for it is God who works in you both to will and to do for His good pleasure" (Phil. 2:12–13 NKJV).

Putting It All Together

Here's the process in a nutshell: when you are saved, you are freed from the grip of sin and are forgiven by God. You still have the *ability* to disobey God and you are still subject to a built-in "bent" toward sinning in particular ways. But as you continue to follow Jesus as your *Lord*, you are sanctified—renewed in your mind, will, and emotions—so you can make consistently right choices and consistently resist temptation. The more you are renewed and become mature in the Lord, the greater the spiritual freedom you will experience and the greater the spiritual strength you will have.

THE CURSE OF THREE TYPES OF SIN

The Bible has a number of passages that link sin directly to a curse. (See Deuteronomy 27:15–26 as one example.) Sin shackles us from following God. It binds us from living out our full potential as human beings. It separates us from God. It keeps us from God's highest and best blessings.

The devil presents sin as something fun and exciting and in some way beneficial to our becoming independent and important. Nothing could be further from the truth. Over time, sin causes decay, loss, and ultimately death. (See Romans 3:23.)

From one perspective, we all live under a generational curse related to sin—it is a curse begun in the Garden of Eden with the sin of Adam and Eve. In the beginning, God created the perfect family and placed them in a perfect setting. God blessed them, gave them everything they needed, and told them to multiply. They walked in the fullness of God's provision until Satan deceived them and they disobeyed. As a result, they lost their dominion over the earth. They lost their paradise.

Adam and Eve experienced the full curse of sin, death, and destruction. The family, as God originally created it, has never been the same since. Every undesirable, hereditary trait that seems to run in the family results directly from the sin of Adam and Eve. We are all born with a propensity to sin in some way, and we can see that certain families also seem marked by sin in particular ways.

Three Terms for Sin

The Bible makes a distinction between the terms *sin*, *iniquity*, and *transgression*. Psalm 32 clearly identifies these three kinds of sin. This psalm was written after David committed adultery with Bathsheba and had her husband, Uriah, sent to certain death at the front lines of military conflict:

Blessed is he whose *transgression* is forgiven,
Whose *sin* is covered.
Blessed is the man to whom the LORD does not impute
iniquity,
And in whose spirit there is no deceit.
When I kept silent, my bones grew old
Through my groaning all the day long.
For day and night Your hand was heavy upon me;
My vitality was turned into the drought of summer.
I acknowledged my *sin* to You,
And my *iniquity* I have not hidden.
I said, "I will confess my *transgressions* to the LORD,"
And You forgave the *iniquity* of my sin.
(PSALM 32:1–5 NKJV, EMPHASIS ADDED)

What brought David to a place of feeling and being blessed—even in the wake of these terrible choices and behaviors in his life? David confessed *all* of his sinfulness to God—he acknowledged not only his sin, but his transgressions and iniquity, and he sought God's mercy and forgiveness.

Confronting Sin

Sin means to miss the mark—it means a person falls below the mark of what God has called that person to do. We all are guilty of missing the mark. The Bible tells us, "For all have sinned; all fall short of God's glorious standard" (Rom. 3:23). Our finite nature alone falls short of God's infinite nature; in addition, we fail repeatedly to live up to the full potential God has placed in us when it comes to our character and motives. Sin is our nature until we are transformed by the Holy Spirit.

Confronting Transgressions

Transgression refers to trespassing or overstepping preestablished boundaries. *Trespasses* and *transgressions* are synonymous terms. We transgress or trespass against man and God. We go beyond the limit of what is allowed. We also trespass against the physical, moral, and psychological boundaries set by other people.

We've all seen "No Trespassing" signs. We "trespass" against people emotionally when we cross a certain line by willfully manipulating them, abusing them, using them selfishly, or ignoring their expressed wishes.

Transgressions are acts—usually what we say or do. We can continue to transgress against our neighbors—and we do— even after we are saved. Jesus taught us to confess our transgressions day by day as part of the model prayer: "Forgive us our trespasses, as we forgive those who trespass against us." (See Matthew 6:12)

Confronting Iniquity

Iniquity means to "bend" or to distort the heart. It implies a certain weakness or predisposition toward a particular type of sin. Sin becomes an iniquity when a person keeps committing the same act. Over time, the practice of a repeated sin becomes spontaneous behavior. Iniquity is *habitual.*

It is the habitual iniquity of a person that is passed down through the generations. Unless something is done to change the sin habit, each generation of offspring adds to the iniquity. The pattern becomes increasingly engrained, and thus, more difficult to break.

The Price Has Been Paid for All Our Sin

The good news is that Jesus bore not only our sin nature, but also our transgressions and iniquities.

*The blood of Jesus Christ his Son cleanseth us from all
sin. (1 John 1:7 KJV)*

*He was wounded for our transgressions, he was
bruised for our iniquities: the chastisement of our peace
was upon him; and with his stripes we are healed.
(Isaiah 53:5 KJV)*

The pattern in the Bible from cover to cover is that blood must
be shed for sins to be remitted. Certainly Jesus shed His blood
on the cross of Calvary and in so doing the Bible tells us He
bore our sin: "For God made Christ, who never sinned, to be
the offering for our sin, so that we could be made right with
God through Christ" (2 Cor. 5:21).

In all, Jesus shed blood eight times:

1. He prayed with such intensity in the Garden of Gethse-
   mane blood came from the pores of his skin.
2. He was beaten with fists as part of being interrogated by the
   high priest, causing bruising or bleeding under the skin.
3. His beard was plucked.
4. A crown of thorns was pressed on His head.
5. His back was ripped open by both flogging and scourging.
6. His hands were nailed to the cross.
7. His feet were nailed to the cross.
8. His side was pierced with a sword.

Eight is the number associated with new beginnings. Jesus
made a full provision for all of our transgressions, iniquities,
and sin—He gave us a fresh start.

Jesus Was Bruised for Our Iniquities

Open wounds and bruises are different. An open wound will
eventually scab over and heal. A bruise, however, can stay

around much longer. It can become discolored and can even go as deep as to bruise the bone. The apostle Paul seemed to have a clear understanding of this when he wrote, "The mystery of iniquity doth already work" (2 Thess. 2:7 KJV). The bruising deep within a person's soul is often not visible to the outside world—it nonetheless is present and painful.

The effects of abuse can leave a person bent toward particular behaviors. Psychological traits—including a wide variety of emotional and mental problems—can run deep, even though a person may excel and achieve in external ways.

King David said, "Behold, I was shapen in iniquity; and in sin did my mother conceive me" (Ps. 51:5 KJV). David wasn't talking about the sexual act of his conception being a sin, but rather that he had inherited the iniquity of his ancestors. Daniel spoke about "the iniquities of our fathers" (Dan. 9:16 KJV). The prophet Jeremiah lamented iniquity: "Our fathers have sinned, and are not; and we have borne their iniquities" (Lam. 5:7 KJV).

INIQUITY IS PASSED DOWN IN FAMILIES

Sin is the nature of human beings—descendants of Adam and Eve. We are born with this sin nature and are subject to it until we accept Jesus Christ as Savior. But it is iniquity we need to address in reversing generational curses and turning them into generational blessings.

This is how the human race became bound up in iniquity: when God created the earth, He set up a basic principle that has never changed—everything reproduces after its own kind. In the natural, if something becomes malformed—for example, the fruit of a tree is not according to its stock, or an animal bears a corruption of some kind—we say that a mutation has taken place. The same is true in the spiritual realm.

Unless there's an intervening factor, uncorrupted living things will produce good fruit, and mutant or corrupted creation will produce corrupt fruit. Jesus noted this in teaching about false prophets. He said, "You will know them by their fruits. Do men gather grapes from thornbushes or figs from thistles? Even so, every good tree bears good fruit, but a bad tree bears bad fruit.... Therefore by their fruits you will know them" (Matt. 7:16–17, 20 NKJV).

A good farmer will do his best to weed out mutations—either to keep the seed from a mutated plant from being planted, or to keep a mutated animal from breeding. This natural practice is also mirrored in the spiritual realm. The Bible gives several very strong examples of God "weeding out" iniquity from human creation.

Canaan, the land to which God called Abraham, was a land of iniquity. The spiritual bloodline of the Canaanites was corrupt and defiled. Their hearts were inclined only to evil. God eventually rained fire and brimstone on two Canaanite cities: Sodom and Gomorrah. These two major enclaves of Canaanite sin were wiped out completely, but other areas occupied by Canaanites remained.

Hundreds of years later, when the Israelites were preparing to reenter Canaan under the leadership of Moses, the Canaanite people still inhabited the land. The Lord told the Israelites through Moses:

> As for the towns of the nations the LORD your God is
> giving you as a special possession, destroy every living
> thing in them. You must completely destroy the Hittites,
> Amorites, Canaanites, Perizzites, Hivites, and Jebusites,
> just as the LORD your God has commanded you. This
> will keep the people of the land from teaching you their
> detestable customs in the worship of their gods, which

would cause you to sin deeply against the LORD your God. (Deuteronomy 20:16–18)

The iniquity of the Canaanites had become so entrenched they had to be completely eliminated in order to destroy their bloodline and keep the Israelites from becoming contaminated with the same iniquity.

There are some people who read statements such as these in the Bible and conclude that God is hard-hearted. Nothing could be further from the truth. At the same time, most people who are the victims of evil desire for evil to be eradicated from the earth. Most people *want* all child abuse, spousal abuse, terrorism, graft, and embezzlement to stop. Evil is not just a vague notion. Evil infects *people*. It manifests itself through human behavior. The Canaanites became so filled with corrupt motives, schemes, and behavior that the elimination of evil could not be fully separated from the elimination of evil people.

God's plan is that those who obey His commands are blessed; those who hate Him, as evidenced by their rebellion and evil deeds, are subject to the curse.

The Israelites did not obey God. They did not eradicate the Canaanites and as a result, iniquity multiplied. Not only did Canaanite evil continue and grow, but it infected Israel— idolatry and worship of false gods became mixed with the pure worship of the one true and living God. In other words, worship became corrupted. Moral and social disciplines established in God's commandments were compromised.

The prophet Ezekiel tells about God's plan to cleanse the bloodline of His people. The ninth chapter of the book of Ezekiel presents a vivid picture of God's command to the angels to slay everyone who didn't have the mark of God on his or her life:

*"Go after him through the city and kill; do not let your
eye spare, nor have any pity.*

*Utterly slay old and young men, maidens and little
children and women; but do not come near anyone on
whom is the mark; and begin at My sanctuary." So they
began with the elders who were before the temple.*

*Then He said to them, "Defile the temple, and fill the
courts with the slain. Go out!" And they went out and
killed in the city.*

*. . . Then He said to me, "The iniquity of the house
of Israel and Judah is exceedingly great, and the land is
full of bloodshed, and the city full of perversity; for they
say, 'The LORD has forsaken the land, and the LORD
does not see!' And as for Me also, My eye will neither
spare, nor will I have pity, but I will recompense their
deeds on their own head." (Ezekiel 9:5–7, 9–10 NKJV)*

God assured the prophet Ezekiel that all would eventually be
well, because in the end—after the judgment had fallen and
only the righteous remained—the generations who would
come from the righteous would serve the Lord. (See Ezekiel
14:22–23.)

Insight from Marilyn

When I was thirty-six years old, I found myself under tremendous pressure. The devil whispered to me, "You are just like
your father. You look and act like him. You are going to have
a nervous breakdown just like he did."

I began to agree, "Yes, I'm just like my father. I probably
am going to have a nervous breakdown, too." At that point,

the Lord spoke to me and reminded me, "I am your Father. You are just like Me, and I've *never* had a nervous breakdown. Neither will you."

The question is this: *whose nature are you believing for?* Do you believe the die has been irrevocably cast and you will be just like your earthly parents or grandparents? Or do you believe you can choose to take after your heavenly Father?

DIVINE INTERRUPTION

*D*ecide whose nature you are going to believe for: do you expect to be just like your parents or grandparents, or just like your heavenly Father? Make a list of the natural traits you want to trade in and write down the corresponding traits God offers you. By faith, receive His best.

4

Outrun What Runs in Your Family

Have you ever heard someone say, "Well, that problem runs in my family"? The person may be talking about a particular weakness or disease, or perhaps a certain vulnerability of some kind.

More and more, we are learning that certain physical ailments certainly do run in families—for example, arthritis, asthma, cancer, obesity, alcoholism, heart conditions, diabetes, digestive tract and kidney problems, and chronic pain.

Emotional and psychological behaviors can also be inherited. Some families seem to be riddled with depression, lust, and anger.

Iniquity is likely at the root of a host of many other things that are negative in a family lineage: sterility, divorce, adultery, rebellion, debt . . . the list can go on and on.

The good news is that God gives you the ability to *outrun* anything that runs in your family!

What Is Your Family Totem?

Primitive people often have an understanding of curses we in the Western world don't. For example, tribal peoples in Zimbabwe, Africa, have what they call *totems.* These totems represent their tribes.

One tribe has a snake as its totem. Every family in this tribe has a little house for its pet snake in the backyard. Now the snake is anything but a "god" in the Bible or in the United States, where the snake is generally regarded as a sneaky, crafty, slimy creature. But in this part of Africa, snakes are considered to be deity.

Many pagan people worship specific animals, reptiles, or other creatures. Very often the *nature* of that particular creature has characteristics evident in the psyche of the tribe worshiping the creature.

We know God cursed the snake because of its role in the fall of man. The Bible names many animals as "unclean." Interestingly, some of these animals are well-known for behaviors we would consider to be negative:

- Lizards are fearful animals—they will move quickly at the slightest movement or noise.
- Bats are creatures of the night.
- Vultures gather where there is death and decay.
- Spiders are territorial and predatory, spinning webs to trap passersby.
- The scorpion inflicts pain that paralyzes its victims.

The tribe with a snake as its totem has a reputation as a deceitful and scheming people. Manipulation is regarded as admirable behavior and the ability to tell a lie and get away with it is also lauded.

Some family trees in our own culture might very well be symbolized by a snake. You may know a family whose history is marked by lies and deception. Manipulation, fearfulness, abuse, shiftiness—any repetitive negative behavior can become a family trait from one generation to the next.

WHO IS RESPONSIBLE FOR ACTING AGAINST INIQUITY?

Who is responsible for acting against iniquity? We are!

The Bible message is a very clear one: if we do not deal with the iniquity in our lives, God eventually will. If we do not clean up our unclean nature, our unclean nature will keep us in a miry pit.

In most cases, God does not act in a supernatural way to eradicate iniquity from a family or a nation. He has given us free will; He allows evil people to wage evil deeds. God removes His hand of blessing and the evil heart of man functions according to its unclean nature.

Don't wait for generational iniquity to run its course in your family tree. Take action now—in your everyday life and in your family.

Insight from Marilyn

My husband, Wally, and I adopted our son, Michael, when he was three-and-a-half years old. Michael was a sweet little boy, but we experienced a number of problems throughout his growing-up years.

When we look back, Wally and I know we made some mistakes in raising Mike, but we also know we did most things right. No parent, of course, ever does *everything* right. Some of our son's problems, however, were entirely opposite of what we modeled before him or taught him. We often asked ourselves, *What is the cause of this? Why is Michael still struggling with these issues?*

It was only as we began to study the insidious impact of generational sin that we realized Mike may have inherited many of his propensities—the bent of iniquity—from his biological family. As his adoptive and spiritual parents, we took authority over these problems in the spiritual realm in order to release him from the generational curse on his life.

One of Mike's difficulties was an addiction to drugs. He has been free of that addiction for many years now. He also struggled with depression. He has been free of that as well. While he may struggle from time to time in certain areas, he is not bound by his bloodline.

Mike has a wonderful capacity for enjoying life. In fact, I dedicated my book *Enjoy Life* to him, because he really is such a joy to be around. Mike is his own person. He has long, thick hair and likes earrings and tattoos. Mike is a beautiful person—he has a heart of gold; he is devoted and discerning; he is the most loving person in our family.

Michael is an excellent father, grandfather, and uncle. I see in him a genuine example of the Bible truth: what the devil means for harm, God can turn to good! (See Genesis 50:20.) Whatever iniquity Mike may have inherited in his bloodline is being turned into a legacy of generational blessing for Mike's children and grandchildren.

IT'S SO IMPORTANT WHOM YOU MARRY!

Because iniquity can be passed down from parent to child, it is extremely important whom you marry, and whom your children marry. Begin the moment your children are born to pray that God will provide godly spouses for them. Just as generational curses can be reversed in a family lineage, so, too, established blessings in a family lineage can be negated. This can happen very dramatically when believers marry unbelievers.

The Bible has a very clear example of this. God gave Abraham tremendous promises for himself and his family. God blessed Isaac, Abraham's son, in wonderful ways. Isaac and Rebekah had two sons: Esau and Jacob. Jacob fully accepted his identity in the Lord and the blessings continued in his family line. Esau, however, did not love and obey the God of his forefathers.

Esau sold his birthright to his brother, but that isn't the most important error he made. The Bible tells us: "Esau saw that the daughters of Canaan did not please Isaac his father. So Esau went to Ishmael and took to be in his wife, [in addition] to the wives he [already] had, Mahalath daughter of Ishmael Abraham's son, the sister of Nebaioth" (Gen. 28:8–9 AMP).

Esau married into the Hittites—in fact, he took two Hittite wives. The Hittites were descendants of the Canaanites. Isaac and Rebekah were grieved over Esau's marrying these two women, because there was a generational curse on the Canaanites that had not been broken.

Bible historians and scholars tell us the Hittites were immoral people. God eventually eliminated the Hittites from the face of the earth. The people, as a tribe, became completely extinct.

The Bible says very strongly in both the Old and New Testaments that the people of God are not to be yoked, or married, to those who do not worship God. The apostle Paul made this clear to the early church in Corinth: "Be ye not unequally yoked together with unbelievers" (2 Cor. 6:14 KJV). Why? Because unbelievers are under the curse of sin.

Does this mean a Christian who marries an unbeliever must live under a curse? No. Does this mean a spouse who accepts Christ after marriage, when the other spouse does not, lives under a curse? No.

Read these verses and be encouraged:

> *If a Christian woman has a husband who is an unbeliever, and he is willing to continue living with her, she must not leave him. For the Christian wife brings holiness to her marriage, and the Christian husband brings holiness to his marriage. Otherwise, your children would not have a godly influence, but now they are set apart for him. (1 Corinthians 7:13–14)*

> *In the same way, you wives must accept the authority of your husbands, even those who refuse to accept the Good News. Your godly lives will speak to them better than any words. They will be won over by watching your pure, godly behavior. (1 Peter 3:1–2)*

One believing mate sanctifies the household. Those who accept Christ are freed from the chains of the past that have bound them. It is only the rebellious who remain under a curse. The children of a union between an unbeliever and a believer are not doomed to live under a generational curse.

The conversation and behavior of a godly man or woman can be a tremendous witness to an unbelieving spouse. If you are unequally yoked to an unsaved mate, ask God to forgive you of any guilt related to your marriage. Then, begin to pray diligently and fervently for your spouse to accept Christ. Be loving—in fact, love so generously as to love "the hell" right out of your spouse's heart! Continue to attend church—with your children. Continue to pray—with your children.

Continue to read and study God's Word—and to share the truths of God's Word with your children.

❧

Insight from Marilyn

For most of his life, my father was opposed to my mother's active faith. My mother wanted to obey God in all things, including tithing. My father gave my mother a specified amount of money for running the household and preparing meals. Without ever saying a word, my mother managed that money so well she was able to tithe to the Lord and still run her home and prepare good meals.

My mother treated my father with respect, but she also made time to pray and to study the Word, no matter how difficult it might have been. She was a wonderful example to me that if a person is truly committed to following the Lord, that person can and will find a way to do so!

I have no doubt it was because of my mother's faithfulness in praying and building her faith on God's Word that my father eventually gave his life to the Lord.

FIVE STEPS TO FREEDOM FROM INIQUITY

There are five steps a person can take to be set free from the generational patterns of iniquity.

Step 1: Acknowledge and Confess the Iniquities of Your Forefathers.

Make a list of every person you know by name in your family tree back to four generations, that is, all the way back to your great-great-grandparents. If you don't know all these names, list as many as you do know.

Then make a second list of those things you believe to be generational curses in your family tree. Identify specific sins, habits, failures, illnesses, mental or emotional problems, or weaknesses and propensities that seem to plague you or your family. It is not necessary for these two lists to be linked; you may not know which flaws or problems were connected to certain people.

Pray over these two lists and ask God to cleanse you of any iniquity that may have been passed down through known and unknown members of your family tree. Ask Him to cleanse you of any iniquity you may have inherited and every form of sin or weakness you have identified as being a possible generational curse.

Step 2: Forgive Your Family Members.

Never harbor a victim mind-set against your family members. They may have passed on a propensity or a bent toward sin, but no family member—alive or in your distant past—truly *makes* you sin. Each of us has the freedom to choose how we will behave.

A family member may have passed on a genetic predisposition to a particular disease, but be encouraged. Scientists tell us that the vast majority of disease we experience is strongly related to our *personal choices*. You may have inherited a weakness toward cancer, for example, but you have a choice as to whether or not you will smoke, what you will eat and drink, how you will exercise, and the amount of stress you will internalize. These behavioral choices are just as potent, or more so, than your genetic predisposition.

Forgive your family members for the role they played in

continuing a pattern of generational sin. Move *forward* toward generational blessing by taking responsibility for your own life.

Forgiveness is vital. It is not a suggestion to Christians—it is a commandment. Jesus said:

> *If you forgive those who sin against you, your heavenly Father will forgive you. (Matthew 6:14)*

> *If you forgive others, you will be forgiven. (Luke 6:37)*

Forgiveness may not happen in an instant. Forgive and keep on forgiving those who have hurt you or influenced you in a negative way. Keep releasing them to God's care.

ℒ

Insight from Marilyn

A number of years ago, we called a man to come and trim some of the bushes in front of our home. They were overgrown and looked bad, so we asked the man to trim them back almost to their stumps. We thought he would take what he cut away to the dump, but instead, he left the trimmings around the bushes. We called and asked him to complete the job, and he did return with his truck. I thought, *Good! The problem is solved.* He did not, however, haul away the trimmings—he bound them into bundles and placed them by the curb. He said, "The trash men will pick them up."

Now, there were five or six very large bundles more than six feet high. I thought, *The trash haulers are going to take one look at all this and say, "Forget it!"*

The next morning I left for work before the trash haulers came. I prayed as I drove, "Lord, surround my trash with favor." I was greatly relieved when I returned home later that day to find all the bundles of bush trimmings gone. I immediately prayed, "Thank You, Lord!"

The Lord spoke to me later that evening and said, "Marilyn, the garbage in a person's life can't be surrounded with favor. I don't grant favor to garbage or cover it with My presence. The only way to get rid of trash is by repenting. Then, and only then, is the trash removed."

God wants us to get rid of all the trash in our lives. We must do our part and He will do His.

Step 3: Confess Your Own Faults, and Ask God to Forgive and Cleanse You.

The devil didn't make you do it. Your forefathers didn't make you do it. What you have done, *you* have done. Own up to your own faults, errors, and sins. The Bible tells us, "People who cover over their sins will not prosper. But if they confess and forsake them, they will receive mercy" (Prov. 28:13).

God's promise is sure:

> *If we are living in the light of God's presence, just as Christ is, then we have fellowship with each other, and the blood of Jesus, his Son, cleanses us from every sin.*
>
> *If we say we have no sin, we are only fooling ourselves and refusing to accept the truth. But if we confess our sins to him, he is faithful and just to forgive us and to cleanse us from every wrong. (1 John 1:7–9)*

Step 4: Submit Your Will to God.

This is the step that truly locks you into freedom from bondage and permanently puts family iniquities in the past. Submission is not robotic. Neither is it a onetime act. Submission is choosing to accept God's plan for your life day by day by day. It is an act of yielding to the guidance of the Holy Spirit. It is saying often, "God, I want to live my life Your way. Help me to do that."

Remember that God's Word tells us: "Continue to work out your salvation with fear and trembling, for it is God who works in you to will and to act according to his good purpose" (Phil. 2:12–13 NIV). *Fear* in this verse refers to an awareness of God's awesome presence. Recognize that God is on your side. He *wants* to help you. He *wants* to guide you into those things that will fulfill His good plan and purpose in your life. He stands with you to save you from all evil—not only in the sense of your eternal spiritual salvation, but also in protecting and preserving you on a daily basis.

The Bible tells us plainly that submission is an act of our will. It is up to us to resist the devil. The really great news is this: when we yield our will to God's will, He enacts His will in our lives. Then, our *will* plus His *power* produces true *willpower*. God-inspired and God-ensured *willpower* is an unbeatable force against temptation!

Ask God daily to empower you to resist the devil and to do the work He has given you to do. Be quick to ask Him to heal you and transform you. Ask Him to renew your mind so you no longer have a sin-consciousness but a righteousness-consciousness—in other words, you are more eager to seek out and do what is right than you are plagued or haunted by temptations to do wrong.

Step 5: Declare Your Faith with the Authority of Jesus' Name.
The name of Jesus is higher than any name.

Devils quiver at his name and angels are launched into flight at His name.

The sick are healed and the oppressed are delivered at His name.

No evil thing can stand against the name of Jesus.

When you speak in the name of Jesus, you are speaking from *inside* the identity of Christ Jesus. You are standing firm in the conviction that Christ is in you and you are in Christ. You are completely covered by the blood of Jesus so nothing of your old nature is evident. Christ is your all in all. This posture positions you for victory!

The Lord tells us we are to ask all things of God in *faith*. In other words, we are to believe that what God has promised for us and to us *will* come to pass. We are asking for what God has already told us is ours to receive.

Therefore, we speak in the name of Jesus and with our faith. All family iniquities must bow to those things addressed by faith in the name of Jesus.

Read what Jesus said about the power of His name:

> *[Jesus said,]* "In my name *they will drive out demons; they will speak in new tongues; they will pick up snakes with their hands; and when they drink deadly poison, it will not hurt them at all; they will place their hands on sick people, and they will get well."* (Mark 15:17–18 NIV, emphasis added)
>
> *[Jesus said,]* "I tell you the truth, my Father will give you whatever you ask *in my name. Until now you have not asked for anything in my name. Ask and you will receive, and your joy will be complete."* (John 16:23–24 NIV, emphasis added)
>
> *[Jesus said,]* "I will do whatever you ask *in my name, so that the Son may bring glory to the Father. You may ask me for anything* in my name, *and I will do it.* (John 14:13–14 NIV, emphasis added)

When you are tempted, immediately ask the Holy Spirit to help you withstand the temptation. Declare *boldly* that the blood of Jesus has cleansed you from sin and iniquity, reconciled you to the Father, and given you victory over all things the devil may try to use against you.

Remind yourself frequently that all generational curses are broken and no longer have power over your life. Remind yourself often that God has all authority over you and He has granted you His name so you might have authority over evil on this earth. Remind yourself that, by shedding His blood, Jesus purchased your freedom from all iniquity.

Be very specific in declaring precisely *what* Jesus has freed you from!

Be very specific in declaring precisely *what* Jesus has authority over!

Speak very specific blessings over yourself and family. Quote the Word of God as words of blessing. Make them a prayer and a bold declaration. Let it be known to all the cosmos that you belong to God and Jesus is your Savior and Lord!

POWER POINT

Through daily obedience—taking just one step of faith at a time—you can reverse the sin and iniquity that once threatened your generations and initiate a pattern of blessing that will outrun what runs in your family . . . and outlast your lifetime.

5

Base Your Family's Future on Truth

W hat is truth?"

Pontius Pilate asked Jesus this question shortly before he ordered Jesus to be crucified.

We don't know what tone of voice Pilate used. Perhaps he asked in dismay, believing truth could not be discovered. Or maybe he asked the question in the hope of hearing a definitive answer. Perhaps he asked philosophically, or with a sarcastic edge, eager for a scholarly discussion or a bitter argument. (See John 18:38.)

What we do know is people continue to ask this question—and in many tones of voice. People today are as puzzled as ever about what is true and what is false.

We also know from the Bible that Pontius Pilate was standing face-to-face with the Source of all truth: Jesus. Jesus said of Himself, "I am the way, the truth, and the life. No one can come to the Father except through me" (John 14:6). Jesus said of the Holy Spirit He would be the "Spirit of truth who goes out from the Father," and the Holy Spirit would "testify" of Jesus (John 15:26 NIV). Jesus said those who followed Him would be people who walked in truth—that the "(fruit of the Spirit is in all goodness and righteousness and truth;) proving what is acceptable unto the Lord" (Eph. 5:9–10 KJV)

As Christians, we can know the truth, believe the truth, speak the truth, and act in a way that is in full agreement with the truth of God. If you sincerely desire to establish a life of blessing for yourself and your family, you *need* truth.

How We Can Know Truth—with Certainty?

How can we know the truth? To build a life on truth means to know Jesus as your personal Savior. It means to follow Him as your Lord. It means to know what He taught and how He lived. It means to model your life—day by day—after Him.

There is a difference between *knowing* Jesus and *knowing about* Jesus. Even the demons know *about* Jesus and believe He is the Son of God. Knowing about someone and knowing a person are two different things. To know somebody means you spend time with that person, communicating often, sharing what is important to you and learning what matters to them.

Knowing Jesus Through Prayer

Jesus wants to hear from you and reveal Himself to you. He does not seek to be a mystery; He *wants* to be known by you.

Why? For starters, to know Him is to love Him! And knowing Him better helps us set the right priorities and follow a prosperous path.

If you will make time for prayer every day, you will learn to recognize the voice of God speaking in your spirit. You may never hear the audible voice of God—or you may. Sometimes, His "voice" is a strong and inescapable idea that seems to fill your entire being, a sudden heightened awareness of something that can be seen or touched, a strong impression, or an intense emotion.

How can you know when you are hearing the voice of the Lord? First, His voice has a simultaneous ring of authority and love that will comfort you. Second, what He says will be in total agreement with God's written Word; it will be directly applicable to your life and family. It will produce benefit if it is obeyed and it will guide you toward a life of blessing.

Insight from Sarah

My husband and I are teaching our children that prayer is not only talking to God, but listening to Him. Every night at the end of our family prayer time, we ask Jesus to tell us anything He wants to tell us. Then we stop to *listen*.

After a few seconds of silence, I ask the children what Jesus is telling them. Sometimes they describe pictures they see in their minds' eyes, and I ask them to describe those pictures. Then I ask them, "What do you think Jesus wants you to know about that picture?" They often come up with responses far beyond their years!

Sometimes they say goofy or questionable things, so I ask them, "Do you think that was God's voice speaking to you, or was that just your own imagination?" If they come up with something I know is contrary to the Word of God, I explain what God's Word says and together, we figure out what the truth is. I know if my children understand when God is speaking to them, it will make an enormous difference in their lives.

These times of prayer are enjoyable, lighthearted, honest, and always beneficial. Not long ago, I misplaced my purse. I looked everywhere for it, to no avail. I had all three children in the car ready to take my daughter, Isabell, to the doctor—but no purse. I finally said to them, "We need to pray Mommy finds her purse!" My son Dave piped up in a very loud voice, "Listen!"

I said, "What, Dave?"

David said, "You need to ask God to show you and then stop and listen to God and He will tell you where it is." He was absolutely right. We prayed. Everybody in the car was quiet. I listened. And sure enough, I felt strongly impressed to call a particular ice cream shop and ask if my purse had been turned in. It had been!

In your prayer time, ask God the questions that weigh heavily on your heart. Ask Him to reveal His solutions to the problems you are facing. Ask Him to show you which steps to take: when, how, and with whom.

Then listen. He is *always* there.

Knowing the Truth through Reading God's Word

One of the best ways to know truth is to read the Word of God daily. It is also one of the best ways to enjoy a blessed life. Bible reading is encouraging and opens our limited minds to the limitless possibilities in God. Reading God's Word calms the soul and can eliminate from our minds and hearts any seeds of evil that might try to take root there.

If you have never read God's Word regularly, start with the Gospels—Matthew, Mark, Luke, and John—the first four books of the New Testament. You will learn about Jesus' life and ministry and see the things He said. Consider getting involved in a Bible study or Sunday school class where you can ask questions and discuss the Scriptures with others. This interaction with others will help you see the practicality of God's Word and apply it to your daily life.

A Heart Ready to Hear and a Mind Ready to Learn

To benefit from the truth, you must be *open* to truth. If you approach a subject—any subject—with a particular prejudice or hardened opinion, you can miss out on hearing *and receiving* something that could change your life for the better.

God's truth is revealed to us over time—ideally from our early years. The Bible says:

> Whom will he teach knowledge?
> And whom will he make to understand the message?
> Those just weaned from milk?
> Those just drawn from the breasts?
> For precept must be upon precept, precept upon precept,
> Line upon line, line upon line,
> Here a little, there a little.
> (ISAIAH 28:9–10 NKJV)

Babies in Isaiah's time were usually not weaned until they were three years old—a child at three is able to hear and understand a great deal. As soon as your child comprehends that words have meaning, begin to read God's Word to him. Find a children's Bible, or a Bible storybook written in simple language. Have a regular story time with your kids. Children *love* having stories read to them. And their tender hearts will be hearing—and receptive to—God's Word.

Line upon Line, Precept upon Precept

The phrase *precept upon precept* refers to the fact that all aspects of God's truth are hinged together. No principle of God stands alone.

The phrase *line upon line* refers to the way in which ancient peoples were taught. In those times, the average person didn't have scrolls or books to consult. All knowledge of God's Word was handed down by word of mouth. Teaching was line by line.

Line by line is still the way people tend to memorize. In fact, we say about an actor learning a part that he is "learning his lines." Hear a line, repeat a line. Read a line, reread the line. Memorize a line, then memorize another line. See and hear the line in context of the full conversation. That's how we learn and memorize line upon line.

Insight from Sarah

My husband, Reece, and I try to have a Bible time with our kids every morning. When that doesn't work out, we try to set aside some other time during the day. We use a children's read-and-learn Bible, but we also familiarize them with an adult version of the Bible so they can gradually become acquainted with the language they will read as they get older.

I will be quick to tell you any time of the day or night that I have three amazing children. They absolutely rock my world!

My daughter Isabell is six years old as I write, but she already loves reading and praying and has memorized several passages of Scripture, including Psalm 23.

My four-year-old son David is very sharp, and also very reflective. He has learned the Lord's Prayer and is working on memorizing Psalm 1. Every night before he goes to bed we tackle just one verse.

Benji is only three, but he is already learning phrases

from the Bible. It won't be long before he is memorizing full verses.

Kids love challenges and they love to excel. Take advantage of their enthusiasm. The more of God's Word they have hidden inside their hearts, the better able they will be to handle the challenges of life—and the more reassurance they will have they are deeply loved by the God who is always with them.

A Lifelong Process

Hearing God's Word is a lifelong process. We learn as we go and we never fully arrive. There are always enriching new insights to be gained and intimate moments with God yet to be experienced. This is the "little by little" Isaiah talked about.

For true learning to take place, information must be encountered repeatedly. The same is true of learning God's ways; we benefit from "soaking" in His Word, from "chewing" on it as we ask Him to reveal what a particular passage means and how it relates to our lives.

At a critical moment in young Joshua's life, God spoke to him some of the most positive, inspiring, and courage-building words in the entire Bible: "Be strong and very courageous. Obey all the laws Moses gave you. Do not turn away from them, and you will be successful in everything you do. Study this Book of the Law continually. Meditate on it day and night so you may be sure to obey all that is written in it. Only then will you succeed" (Josh. 1:7–8).

TRUTH PRODUCES GOOD DECISIONS

A life built on God's truth becomes the foundation for generational blessing because knowledge of the truth empowers us to make *habitual* choices that are in line with the Word of God and the character of Christ.

God honors righteousness.

God rewards those who diligently seek Him.

He blesses choices and decisions that honor Him.

A family *can* choose to follow God and be blessed by God—generation after generation after generation. A family can choose to obey God, receive God's forgiveness, and become the very embodiment of God's blessings to the world.

A family who believes and lives the truth will be *blessed*. Sadly, a family who fails to value truth or refuses to receive truth will eventually reap negative consequences.

Prize the truth . . . seek the truth . . . reap truth's glorious harvest!

Insight from Marilyn

One couple in our church clearly walk in the blessing of God, in turn blessing others, including our church and ministry.

The legacy of blessing did not begin with them but continues in their children's and grandchildren's lives because, as a family, they have honored God over the decades.

Doug and Linda have five sons. At one point, all five sons worked in the family's automobile business. The financial blessing marking their lives goes back to 1926 when Doug's father began working in a Dodge dealership.

He was an honest man with a strong work ethic. After years as a faithful employee, Stanley moved his family to New Mexico and in 1949 he bought his first store—a dealership of his own. The business was successful for a New Mexico location at that time, selling about seven cars each month.

Doug drove the dealership's parts truck in those days. Like his dad, he was a hard worker. The family continued to prosper and during Doug's college years, his dad established another dealership for Doug to run. It became the seed for much more to come.

In 1962, Doug returned to the car business after a stint in the army. He had married Linda in 1960. In 1963, their first child was born and in 1965 the family moved to Denver and continued in the car business.

Over time, one successful dealership became several thriving auto stores. Today, in addition to the dealerships, the family owns two concerns in the South—a collision firm and a plant that stores and preps cars sold by the Denver dealerships. With 255 employees and a solid reputation in the community, Doug and Linda have much to be thankful for.

How can one family go so far and experience so much good? It's not by accident. Doug and Linda were raised by loving parents who instilled in their children solid values. Linda was raised in the Methodist church and was born again as a young girl. Doug was born again in college when a young football player involved with Campus Crusade for Christ shared the gospel with him at a fraternity house. Doug and several others then got involved with Campus Crusade for Christ and held weekly evangelistic meetings. The ministry's outreach increased greatly during the time of Doug's involvement.

Today, Doug and Linda are a great blessing to our church and ministry and have touched many lives through their faithfulness and generosity. They are people who make it a practice to sow goodness into others' lives. The couple's five children are also prosperous and have families of their own.

When talking about blessing, Doug is quick to share about tithing. Back in New Mexico in 1972, a couple with four young daughters invited Doug and Linda to breakfast. The couple wanted to talk to them about tithing. They explained the principles of the tithe and challenged Doug and Linda to begin to give a tenth. Doug and Linda accepted the challenge and have been tithing ever since—including paying tithes on the dealerships' finances.

It's no wonder this family enjoys generational blessing—they were mentored by moral parents and caring friends. They are teachable and open to the Spirit of God, always sowing God's Word into the lives of others. They are faithful tithers and financially support other ministries. They are honest in business and known for their integrity. They expect their employees to do the same. They have raised five wonderful children who are wise and prosperous and who operate in integrity, glorifying God.

As a family, they have chosen truth. They have honored their heavenly Father in all their ways, including the firstfruits and the tithe, and He is honoring and blessing them and their generations!

THE TREMENDOUS PRIVILEGE WE HAVE IN CHOOSING TRUTH

You can choose to spend time with Jesus, and how closely you will listen to Him and obey what He tells you. You can choose what you will take into your mind and heart. You can choose what you believe. You have a free will to make countless choices and decisions every day.

Because of this amazing gift—the God-given freedom to *choose*—we have the privilege to *choose* lives of blessing for ourselves and our families. Even if you didn't have the benefits of growing up the way Doug and Linda did, even if you come from a long line of hard-core sinners, you can *choose* a life that will bring blessing upon you, your children, and your grandchildren. God's Word tells us:

Today I am giving you the choice between a blessing and a curse! You will be blessed if you obey the commands of the LORD your God that I am giving you today. You will receive a curse if you reject the commands of the LORD your God and turn from his way by worshiping foreign gods. (Deuteronomy 11:26–28)

If you will obey God's commands—not just giving lip service, but actually doing what pleases Him—you are promised great things. "If you fully obey the LORD your God by *keeping all the commands I am giving you* today, the LORD your God will exalt you above all the nations of the world. You will experience all these blessings if you obey the LORD your God" (Deut. 28: 1–2, emphasis added).

Our obedience *always* puts us in line for God's *best*!

Insight from Marilyn

The power of choice is an amazing one. Every day, we each are faced with a thousand opportunities—or more!—to choose what we will think, what we will say, and what we will do. To choose to do nothing is still a choice.

If you don't like something in your life today, choose something better.

If something is broken in your life, choose to fix it.

If something isn't producing the result you want, make a change.

God has given you the power of choice and the ability to seek out and know the truth.

He has invited you to enjoy and to pass on His very choicest blessings *in this life*. And when your work here is done, He has invited you to live with Him—*forever*!

DIVINE INTERRUPTION

In your prayer time, ask God the questions that weigh heavily on your heart. Ask Him to reveal His solutions to the problems you are facing. Ask Him to show you which steps to take: when, how, and with whom.

Then listen.

6

Develop a Faith Worth Passing On

God is always looking for *faith*.

It is our faith that triggers God to act on our behalf.

It is our faith in God that allows us to overcome and reverse generational curses.

It is our faith that brings God's blessings into our lives.

The great "faith chapter" in the Bible is Hebrews 11. There are two main experiences in the life of Abraham, who has been called the "father of all who have faith," worthy our special attention here as we seek to establish a life and lineage of blessing. God challenges us to use our faith in the same two ways He challenged Abraham:

1. God challenges us to trust Him for our unseen future.
2. God challenges us to trust Him to bless our children.

TRUST GOD FOR YOUR FUTURE

Abraham is cited as noteworthy by the author of the book of Hebrews because he "obeyed and went, even though he did not know where he was going" (Heb. 11:8 NIV).

The writer of Hebrews tells us:

> And even when he reached the land God promised him, he lived there by faith—for he was like a foreigner, living in a tent. And so did Isaac and Jacob, to whom God gave the same promise. Abraham did this because he was confidently looking forward to a city with eternal foundations, a city designed and built by God. (Hebrews 11:9–10)

What is really being said here?

Abraham was willing to go *wherever* God told him because he believed what God promised him about his own life and future. He did not see in order to believe. He believed that he might see—even if he had only a glimpse of the future to come.

Abraham did not know . . . and then believe. He believed that he might know.

Abraham did not possess . . . and then believe. He believed that he might one day possess.

This is the very essence of faith. We believe God for what we do not yet see based upon who God is, not on what we have. Faith moves us forward. Faith compels us to look into the future and into eternity and see our descendants there. It compels us to look into the future and believe for God's best to unfold before our eyes, in spite of the setbacks we may have experienced so far.

Your faith lays claim to generational blessings. The eyes of your faith can "see" your children serving God. Your prayers of faith will lay the groundwork for your children to prosper in every way.

"But I just can't believe for all that," you may be saying.

Yes, you can!

God says in His Word He has imparted to *every* person a measure of faith. The more you dare to believe God, the easier it will be to *believe* God. The more you put your faith into action and live in a way that demonstrates your faith, the more your faith drives your actions.

Abraham is known for going to a place of promise without having any idea where it was. He didn't know the longitude and latitude or the geographical features of the land he was about to walk, but he was confident he would know when he arrived. He was going to a city built by *God*.

Your Faith Influences Others Around You

The faith of Abraham in believing God to show him the unseen became a contagious faith. Probably the first person who caught that faith was Sarah, who needed faith to receive God's extraordinary promise to her and her husband. The writer of Hebrews says: "By faith, barren Sarah was able to become pregnant, old woman as she was at the time, because she believed the One who made a promise would do what he said" (Heb. 11:11 MSG).

Your faith will influence your spouse, even an unbelieving spouse. Your faith can free your spouse to trust God more fully and in many cases, it will compel your spouse to seek God's direction more intentionally.

Your faith will influence your children. Even if your spouse is faithless, you can influence your children in matters of truth, faith, and obedience.

Your faith is good, strong spiritual seed. It will weather storms, it will survive times of drought, it will come up in hard ground, it will produce abundant fruit—if you will *plant it*. Don't wait for the conditions to be perfect; allow your faith to touch your loved ones even when it feels as though all hell is breaking loose around you.

ENTRUST YOUR CHILD TO GOD'S LOVE

The second thing the writer of Hebrews noted about Abraham was that Abraham trusted God with his son Isaac. "It was by faith that Abraham offered Isaac as a sacrifice" (Heb. 11:17).

The Bible is clear: this was a test God sent into Abraham's life. God was not testing Abraham to find out if Abraham had faith—He was allowing Abraham to face a test so Abraham could discover just how much his faith had grown! And, from this experience, Isaac's faith would be developed and would guide *his* life.

Giving Your Child to the Lord Always *Takes Faith*

It took great faith for Abraham to offer his son Isaac to God. It takes no less faith for parents today to give up their sons and daughters to God's care.

How many parents do you know who believe the salvation of their sons or daughters is dependent upon what they say and do . . . or believe the financial welfare of their sons or daughters is dependent upon what they provide or recommend as a career . . . or believe they know better than anyone what will bless their children? To trust God with your children—to realize that in spite of your responsibility as a parent, God is your children's ultimate provider and protector—can be challenging. It means letting go so God can take hold. It means giving up what you want so God might express what He wants.

Abraham did not sacrifice his son blindly. He believed his son was going to be the first known person to be resurrected from the dead. Abraham believed God's promise that many generations of heirs were going to be produced through Isaac. The writer of the book of Hebrews confirms this, saying:

It was by faith that Abraham offered Isaac as a sacrifice when God was testing him. Abraham, who had received God's promises, was ready to sacrifice his only son, Isaac, though God had promised him, "Isaac is the son through whom your descendants will be counted." Abraham assumed that if Isaac died, God was able to bring him back to life again. And in a sense, Abraham did receive his son back from the dead. (Hebrews 11:17–19)

The writer of the book of Hebrews is looking back on Abraham's example *after the resurrection of Jesus.* He sees what Abraham did as a figure—a symbolic representation or foreshadowing of what God would one day do in and through Jesus. Abraham offered Isaac. God responded by giving Isaac back his life. God offered Jesus. God then responded by giving Jesus back His life.

God does not ask you to entrust your children to Him without holding out to you the all-encompassing hope that He will fulfill your children's lives in ways that will bring Him the greatest glory and give you and your children the greatest joy.

Take some time to reflect on that truth. To entrust your child fully to the Lord is to claim, by your faith, that:

- God loves your child with an everlasting love.
- God's purposes for creating your child are going to be fulfilled.

- Your child's life is going to count for eternity.

We can—we must trust God to do *His* work in our children. But what about your grown children?

Abraham entrusted Isaac to God when Isaac was a *grown child*. Isaac may very well have been nearly thirty years old at the time of the sacrifice recorded in Genesis 22. Some Bible scholars believe Isaac was exactly the same age Jesus was when Jesus died on the cross. Isaac certainly was more than twelve years old, the age at which boys become men in the Hebrew tradition. Isaac was an adult child.

If you have been holding your grown children in the clutches of your own dreams, hopes, and desires, let go. Trust God. Let your grown children know you are entrusting their lives to the Lord completely.

Do the same when it comes to your family. Trust God to give you the family He desires for you to have. Then trust God to form your children into the persons they were designed to be. Trust God to build character and strong faith into the fabric of your children's personalities. Trust God to lay the foundations of your children's lives so they never crumble, but always remain firm throughout your child's life.

Never Stop Believing!
Should a parent ever quit trusting God for the salvation of an adult child? *Never.*

When Moses was just a few days old, his parents took a bold *faith action*. They confronted the law of the land and took steps to hide their infant son from Pharaoh, who ordered the death of every male Israelite baby. Actually, Amran and Jochebed, Moses' parents, followed the *letter* of the law. They threw their baby son into the Nile River just as Pharaoh ordered. However, they defied the spirit of the law. They tucked their baby son into a tiny boat *before* they threw him *and the boat* into the river.

God honored the faith of these parents and arranged for Pharaoh's daughter to hear the cries of the baby at just the right time. This daughter adopted Moses and subsequently raised and educated him in Pharaoh's court.

At the time Moses was plucked from the river by Pharaoh's daughter, Moses' older sister Miriam made a suggestion about a woman who might be able to nurse the baby for Pharaoh's daughter. That nursing woman, of course, was Moses' own mother. For the first three years of Moses' life, Jochebed nursed her son with the blessing of Pharaoh. Isn't it amazing how God can orchestrate our lives when we trust Him to do so?

Jochebed did not only nourish her son physically. As any good Israelite woman would have done, she told her son about God and about who he was as a Hebrew child in Jehovah's care.

"But Moses was only a baby," you may be saying.

Yes, but the spirit is alive in us from our conception. We each have a foundation of information imparted to us long before we ever understand language or are able to speak words. Jochebed spoke into Moses' life what could be heard in his spirit, and what would be lasting and unshakeable in his life. She spoke words of faith to her infant son, and those words never left him.

Moses was forty years old when he stood up for who he was as a Hebrew man. His actions resulted in his exile; Moses was eighty years old before he came face-to-face with God at the burning bush, where he made a decision to follow God wherever God might lead him and to do whatever God might ask of him. By faith, Moses led the children of Israel out of Egypt and toward their land of promise. (See Hebrews 11:23–29.)

Amran and Jochebed very likely did not live to see Moses become the man of faith who led Israel out of bondage in Egypt. But that's real faith—they did not see and then believe. They believed for what they had not yet seen—and they never stopped believing.

Your child may not make a decision for Christ or fully surrender his entire future to Christ until later in life. You may not live to see the day, but you can believe for that day nonetheless.

PASSING ON YOUR FAITH LESSONS

Of all the things Abraham did in his life—and all the ways in which he manifested faith—the writer of Hebrews picks out these two instances. Why? Because they are the foremost challenges of our lives, too.

We each face the challenge of trusting God with what we don't know about our own future. We each face the challenge of trusting God to work in the lives of those we love. It is only when we are willing to trust God with what we cannot see and cannot know—and only when we are willing to trust God completely with our children—that God puts us into position to teach about faith with full authority.

Consider the aftermath of what happened in the lives of Abraham and Isaac.

Do you think for a moment Isaac ever forgot that day on Mount Moriah when his father, Abraham, trusted God to the point of being willing to sacrifice him, only to have God honor that act of faith with a substitute ram caught in a thicket of thorns nearby? Never!

Do you think Isaac ever forgot anything Abraham told him about trusting God from that day forward?

Do you think Isaac had a deeper desire to know God as his father did?

Do you think Isaac had a deeper capacity to trust God for his own life?

Absolutely!

Abraham was not only a man of faith, but he became a role model of faith because he was willing to go wherever and do whatever, according to God's Word to him. Abraham was in position to pass on his faith *because he exhibited his faith fully to his child.*

The Bible tells us that is precisely what happened. "By faith Isaac blessed Jacob and Esau concerning things to come" (Heb. 11:20 KJV).

Did Jacob pass on what Isaac modeled and taught him? The Bible says: "By faith Jacob, when he was a dying, blessed both the sons of Joseph; and worshipped, leaning upon the top of his staff" (Heb. 11:21 KJV).

Did Joseph pass on the faith lessons he learned from his father and saw modeled by his father? The Bible says: "By faith Joseph, when he died, made mention of the departing of the children of Israel; and gave commandment concerning his bones" (Heb. 11:22 KJV).

Faith lessons were passed down from generation to generation to generation. The Bible declares to us today: "The real children of Abraham, then, are all those who put their faith in God" (Gal. 3:7). When we live by faith, we are the spiritual children of Abraham.

What is the point of receiving any type of lesson? So you can learn and apply that lesson to your own life, with equal or even better results. This is especially true of faith lessons.

Be quick to share with your children how God has honored your acts of faith in the past. Be quick to tell them how you have lived by faith, and with what results. Pass the faith lessons of your life on to your children.

Tell of God's Miracle-Working Power

Always be quick to share with your children and others the miracle-working power of God in your life.

Several years ago a man in our church was diagnosed with incurable bone marrow cancer. Up to that point Bob appeared to be a very healthy man. He was a "guy's guy"— a former college wrestler who had worked as a Hollywood stuntman for about ten years. He played soccer at least three times a week, worked out regularly, did hard physical labor in the demolition company he founded, and was very active. When he was diagnosed with this disease, he asked doctors to hit it as hard as they could. Bob was prepared for a fight.

The physicians at the Mayo Clinic suggested Bob have a bone marrow transplant, and he agreed to this procedure. He began chemotherapy to prepare him for transplant and in the aftermath of his first chemo treatment, Bob had a serious seizure. He ended up in ICU for more than six weeks, and during the first five of those weeks, the outlook was grim.

The church began to pray in a powerful way for Bob, and his wife and brother-in-law were in nearly round-the-clock prayer for him. During their prayer time, both Bob's wife and brother-in-law had a vision of angels ministering to Bob. That greatly boosted their faith, and the faith of others who walked through this difficult time with them.

During the weeks Bob was in ICU, physicians told the family repeatedly Bob had very little chance of recovery. One physician said he was 9.5 out of ten on the critically ill scale. Another said he had only a 1 percent chance of living. Another said he had only a one-in-a-million chance. Every time the family got this type of news, they doubled their prayers.

The family kept praise music playing around the clock in Bob's room. They anointed him with oil and read the Bible aloud to him. They refused to allow any negative discussion of his condition to be voiced in his room. They recited healing verses over him at least three to four times a day. They fought in the spirit for Bob's life.

Then on the forty-third day Bob was in ICU, his daughter went to his bedside and Bob responded to her—it was the first time he had shown any response. Every day after that, Bob became better. Slowly but surely, the dialysis was stopped, the pneumonia cleared up, his fever went away, the tracheotomy tube was removed, and he began to regain the ability to walk and then talk. Several weeks later, he was released from the hospital and in the months that followed, he began eating normally, exercising, and all the while, drawing closer to God. The cancer was still there, however, and Bob was still planning to undergo the marrow transplant.

The transplant failed—from a medical perspective. But from the faith perspective, God's healing power succeeded. Bob began to improve, week by week, month by month. Sixteen months after Bob was diagnosed with incurable cancer and given only a short time to live, physicians told him to take four months off from all treatment and tests. Why? His blood reports were *normal*. One of the physicians said, "You're starting to make believers out of all of us."

What a mighty God we serve!

His miraculous power never ceases!

Today, Bob and his wife minister to others through a small group. Their harvest of victory has enabled them to sow seeds of victory in the lives of others.

What do you need from God today in your life? Let

miracle-working stories boost your faith to believe what God has done for others, He can and will do for you. Then *your* testimony will be the match that will ignite the faith of another person to believe God for a miracle.

Insight from Marilyn

One of the saddest things that can ever happen to a parent is to experience the death of a child. The natural order of things seems to be violated any time a child precedes a parent in death.

I believe it is important to address the death of children as we discuss generational blessings, because many parents regard the death of a baby or child as a curse. They believe their family blessing has somehow been curtailed by the death of a child.

Even if a child dies, God's purposes are no less fulfilled and His love is not in the least diminished for either you or your child. God will see to it that the *death* of that child brings Him glory—and the way it will do so is threefold. First, the child is immediately and eternally in God's presence, in the fullness of character and identity God instilled in the child from its conception. The child is praising God and fulfilling God's plan for him—now, and forever.

Second, a parent can take joy he will one day be reunited with the child in heaven and live with the child for all eternity. King David said after the loss of a baby son, "I shall go to him, but he shall not return to me" (2 Samuel 12:23).

Third, the child will bring God glory as the parents reflect to the world around them their firm belief: "Even in this, God is worthy of our praise. He is Lord of all. He is trustworthy in all things. We may not understand why certain things happen, but we can know with full assurance, deep in our eternal spirits, that God always acts for our ultimate and eternal benefit." The parents who reflect that attitude to the world are parents who bring glory to God.

Generational blessing is not for this life alone. Generational blessing extends into eternity! The child who dies and is in the near presence of the Lord is an heir of yours in heaven. Ultimately, that's what all parents desire for their children, grandchildren, great-grandchildren, and all subsequent generations.

The child who has died is already fulfilling the ultimate generational blessing—he is living an everlasting blessing in the near presence of God.

Insight from Sarah

I am keenly aware of the faith heritage I have been given and of the responsibility my husband and I have as parents to pass that faith heritage on to our children.

I also know this about faith: I am responsible for the way in which I choose to believe or trust God in every situation I face. My parents certainly have modeled a life of faith for me—and in a way that was vibrant, appealing, and alive. My husband, Reece, models a life of faith. But in the end, how I choose to use my faith—or not use it—is a personal decision I must make.

Yes, our faith choices are our responsibility, but what an awesome privilege it is to make those choices. As we exercise our faith and grow in our faith, we get to enjoy the magnificent harvest that faith yields!

* * *

Faith is contagious. The greatest lesson of faith you can pass on to your own children is the example of faith they see daily in your life. Your children will see your faith, feel your faith, and hear your faith—in turn, they will repeat your words of faith and model your works of faith.

If you give thanks often for good things that come your way, your children who overhear you will learn to do the same.

If you give praise to God for His presence in your life, your children who overhear you praising God will also praise Him.

If you pray and trust God for what you need every day, your children who hear you pray with faith will pray and trust God for what they need.

If you are faithful in reading God's Word, your children who see you reading your Bible or see a well-worn Bible on your nightstand will also want to read the Bible faithfully.

Your children and grandchildren are watching you far more than you may know. Let them see your faith in action!

POWER POINT

Faith allows us to confront the big picture of our eternal future, which cannot be compared to the postage-stamp-sized picture of our earthly past. Therefore living by faith compels us to look into the future and believe for God's best for our family, despite any missteps or failings up till now.

7

Cross Over from *I Can* to *I Must*

When you develop a faith grounded in the truth of Jesus Christ, you are equipped to be an agent of change for your generations. But, to be fully effective, your "equipment" must be field-tested—in other words, your faith must be applied to real situations—*by you.*

This is where the proverbial rubber meets the road in the life of every believer. We must ask ourselves, *Am I willing, as an act of my faith, to do what God tells me to do so I can be free of "my daddy's demons" and create a new legacy for my generations?*

Our good friend, Pastor Jack Hanes from Australia, explains this critical decision-making process in terms of crossing over from the realization that we *can* do something to the revelation that we *must* do it.

When the devil reminds you of your family history, your past failures, or your shortcomings, his parting words will be: "You can't. You can't change. You can't trust God. You can't win." If you accept his prognosis, you have agreed to the status quo in your life and nothing will change, at least not for the better.

However, the apostle Paul, in his letter to the Philippians, declared an opposite truth. He said it is within the believer's power to overcome, whatever the difficulty. "I have learned the secret of living in every situation, whether it is with a full stomach or empty, with plenty or little. For I can do *everything* with the help of Christ who gives me the strength I need" (Phil. 4:12–13, emphasis added).

The shift from the *I can't* mentality to the realization that in Christ *I can* marks the starting line of the faith walk. Suddenly, what we thought was impossible becomes doable, and hope for the future surges!

However, the deeper dimension of the life of faith—the place of real victory—is reached when we move beyond the belief that *I can* and assume the position of *I must*. Yes, *I can* have the victory over the issues that have plagued my family for generations; but *I must* do whatever it takes to be an agent of change. Yes, through prayer *I can* change the circumstances we face; but *I must* pray.

It is easy to understand what we *must do* while listening to the Sunday sermon or meditating on God's Word. But, when the pressures of life hit us head-on, will we stick with God's commands or veer off onto an easier path? Are we truly committed to do what God says we must do, or do we see God's commands as a menu of suggestions from which we get to choose our preferences? Your future, and the future of your family, rests on your answer.

BREAK OUT OF THE STARTING GATE

God doesn't pull punches when it comes to His will for the family; He gives us all the knowledge and power we need to be blessed and He expects us to run with what He has provided.

"Wow," you say, "this is more than I can handle. I'm up to my neck in challenges. I finally reached *I can* mode, but I'm stuck there and I don't know where to begin to dig out."

You've already begun. When *I must* becomes your goal, the door to victory is about to swing wide open. The *I must* approach to God's commands moves you from the complacent to the compelling. When you say to yourself, *I must*, you are placing yourself in the grip of something greater, something beyond you and your ability.

Suddenly, conventional thinking—and the limitations it imposes—are cast off. You have stepped into the jet stream of fourth-dimension living, the place where God's grace puts you over the top and God's best can be manifested in your life.

Jesus Is Our Example

We see that as a young boy, Jesus had a strong sense of what He *must* do. He recognized the greater purpose of His life and focused on doing things that advanced His mission. In this way, He lived up to the expectations of the Father, rather than the expectations of others.

Do you remember when twelve-year-old Jesus went missing on the trip back from Jerusalem? For three harrowing days, Joseph and Mary searched for their boy, until they found Him in the temple.

After three days they found Him in the temple, sitting in the midst of the teachers, both listening to them and

*asking them questions. And all who heard Him were
astonished at His understanding and answers. So when
they saw Him, they were amazed; and His mother said
to Him, "Son, why have You done this to us? Look,
Your father and I have sought You anxiously."*

*And He said to them, "Why did you seek Me? Did
you not know that* I must *be about My Father's business?" But they did not understand the statement which
He spoke to them. (Luke 2:46–50 NKJV, emphasis added)*

Years later, Jesus remained focused on His mission: to save
mankind, including the gentiles, from their sin.

*I am the good shepherd; and I know My sheep, and am
known by My own. As the Father knows Me, even so I
know the Father; and I lay down My life for the sheep.
And other sheep I have which are not of this fold; them
also I must bring, and they will hear My voice; and
there will be one flock and one shepherd. (John 10:14–
16 NKJV, emphasis added)*

You Can Cross Over into I Must Territory

Jesus is the *perfect* example, but He is not our only example
of obedience. The prophet Jeremiah expressed his commitment to God—his recognition of *I must*—this way:

> But if I say, "I will not mention him
> or speak any more in his name,"
> his word is in my heart like a fire,
> a fire shut up in my bones.
> I am weary of holding it in;
> indeed, *I cannot.*
> (JEREMIAH 20:9 NIV, EMPHASIS ADDED)

Jeremiah crossed over the line from *I can* serve God to *I must* serve God. He knew that, even if he wanted to quit, he was compelled by the fire of God burning within to continue in obedience to God.

How badly do you want to see God's best for your family? Will you step across the chasm of indecision and declare that you are compelled to do what God asks? If you do, your faith will find application to real-life situations and everything you see will be subject to change for the better. It's a matter of taking that critical first step and refusing to turn back.

DEVELOP A LIVING FAITH

In the Bible, James takes the air out of any lofty, religious ideas we might have about faith. James makes it clear our faith is designed for practical, everyday living. He contrasts this pragmatic faith with a counterfeit he calls "dead and useless."

> *It isn't enough just to have faith. Faith that doesn't show itself by good deeds is no faith at all—it* is dead and useless.
> *Now someone may argue, "Some people have faith; others have good deeds." I say, "I can't see your faith if you don't have good deeds, but I will show you my faith through my good deeds."*
> *Do you still think it's enough just to believe that there is one God? Well, even the demons believe this, and they tremble in terror! Fool! When will you ever learn that faith that does not result in good deeds is useless? (James 2:17–20, emphasis added)*

To paraphrase James, dead faith is hollow—it's all talk and no action. It stretches to the border of *I can* but stops short of the *I must* zone where faith compels us to act.

James delivered this straightforward faith message without apology. God loves us enough to expose us to the truth and inoculate us against the pitfalls of disobedience. He urges us to obey Him so we might experience His best. As a loving Father, He develops within us the kind of faith that stirs us to say *I must*.

When you are raising children, you expect them to do what you ask, because you want the very best for them. You work hard to protect them from danger. You take the time to explain why you feel so strongly about their choices. You speak plainly in words they can understand so you are sure they have received the benefit of your guidance. And you repeat your instructions as often as necessary, until you see the desired results.

Consider the story of the mother whose five-year-old frayed her last nerve. He didn't seem to get it; no matter how many times she warned him to walk and not run down the stairs, he ran down anyway—and with an armload of toys for good measure.

Exhausted, the mother got down on her knees, put both hands on her son's shoulders, and looked him straight in the eye. She said, "Jimmy, you know Mommy doesn't want you to get hurt, right?"

"Yes, Mom."

"I've told you again and again to walk down the stairs and I've explained to you *why* it is important to obey Mommy, but you don't seem to be paying attention. Can you tell me why you're not listening to me?"

Jimmy looked at his mother with tears welling up in his eyes. "I am listening to you, Mom. It's just that I forget when I'm in a hurry to get downstairs and play."

Jimmy may have had the best of intentions, but he never actually *did* what his mother asked of him. He was focused on other priorities and they diverted his attention from what was truly important. Sometimes we are like Jimmy. We say, "Yes, God. I will do that," but we never get around to *doing it*. For whatever reason—procrastination, forgetfulness, insecurity, fear—we remain frozen in *I can* mode. In time, inaction sentences us to spiritual imprisonment in a place where all we can do is dream about what we *can* do *when* we find the time.

Yes, God has given us His grace and the freedom to choose, but there are some things we simply *must* do. If we neglect them, the dreams we hold dear will be dashed and God's best will pass us by.

ESTABLISH *I MUST* PRIORITIES

The reality of life is this: there will always be multiple priorities vying for our attention. Nevertheless, one thing is paramount—to keep our focus on God. It is the single most important thing we do and it makes the rest of our lives *work*. Jesus said it this way:

> *Your heavenly Father knows that you need all these [other] things. But* seek first the kingdom of God and His righteousness, *and all these things shall be added to you. Therefore do not worry about tomorrow, for tomorrow will worry about its own things. Sufficient for the day is its own trouble. (Matthew 6:32–34 NKJV, emphasis added)*

When you are overwhelmed by mounting demands upon your time and energy, pause and refocus. Look to God; ask Him for wisdom in setting priorities. Then allow Him to lift from your shoulders the self-imposed burden to do it all. You are not called to fret and it's not up to you to make things happen. Your part is simply to seek God *first*.

Meet the Condition and Receive the Promise by Faith

As with anything of spiritual value, faith is the key to receiving. But what happens when your faith is sagging? Are you disqualified from being blessed? No! When your store of faith seems depleted, return to your Source. Those whom we consider to be the strongest in faith rely heavily on the Father to fortify and guide them. God is just fine with that: His Word urges us to come to Him with all of our needs.

> *Now that we know what we have—Jesus, this great High Priest with ready access to God—let's not let it slip through our fingers. We don't have a priest who is out of touch with our reality. He's been through weakness and testing, experienced it all—all but the sin. So let's walk right up to him and get what he is so ready to give. Take the mercy, accept the help. (Hebrews 4:14–16 MSG)*

Take hold of God's grace. Trust Him to shape your will and you will experience the same joy described by the psalmist who found happiness following God's commands: "I inherited your book on living; it's mine forever—what a gift! And how happy it makes me! I concentrate on doing exactly what you say—I always have and always will" (Ps. 119:111–112 MSG).

THE GENERATIONAL POWER OF *I MUST*

Don't underestimate the power God has invested in you to reverse every curse in your family and touch a generation of those outside your household. Don't overlook or second-guess the things He asks you to do. Remember that however mundane His request may seem, what God asks of you is integral to a bigger picture. And obedience to God will yield results exceeding the limits of your imagination.

The story of Queen Esther is a story of simple obedience. In Esther's time, many Jews had been displaced and were living in Persia.

After a bitter dispute between the Persian king, Xerxes, and his wife, Vashti, the queen was deposed. Several years later, King Xerxes held a kind of beauty contest to recruit new wives. Among those chosen was Hadassah, who was given the Persian name *Esther*, meaning "star."

Sometime later, Esther's cousin Mordecai, who worked in the palace, was ordered by the kingdom's number-two man, Haman, to bow down before him. As a faithful Jew, Mordecai refused to bow before anyone but God.

Enraged, Haman convinced the king, who was unaware of Esther's Jewish ancestry, to kill all the Jews living in Persia. Mordecai sent word to Esther of Haman's plot and asked her to appeal to the king on behalf of the Jews. At first Esther refused, because an uninvited approach to the king could have led to her own death. Mordecai urged Esther to reconsider, saying:

> *Don't think for a moment that you will escape there in the palace when all other Jews are killed. If you keep quiet at a time like this, deliverance for the Jews will arise from some other place, but you and your relatives will die.* What's more, who can say but that you have been elevated to the palace for just such a time as this? *(Esther 4:13–14, emphasis added)*

Mordecai's words provoked Esther. Suddenly, she realized why she had been given access to the king in the first place—

she was called by God to save her people. It was an *I must* moment for the queen. She submitted to God's call and it changed everything.

> *Then Esther sent this reply to Mordecai: "Go and gather together all the Jews of Susa and fast for me. Do not eat or drink for three days, night or day. My maids and I will do the same. And then, though it is against the law, I will go in to see the king. If I must die, I am willing to die." So Mordecai went away and did as Esther told him. (Esther 4:15–17)*

Esther called a fast, a time to seek God's heart in this critical matter, but she had already decided to do what she could to save her Jewish family. In the end, the king was persuaded and instead of a generation of Jews being executed, Haman was hung on the gallows.

Once Esther decided she *must* save her people at all cost, God used her to unravel the enemy's plot. When we follow God's direction, our potential is limitless. We can expect to perform tremendous feats—in our families and in our world—for His glory.

Insight from Marilyn

One of the greatest examples I know of two people who turned the world upside down is that of my friends T.L. and the late Daisy Osborn. I had lunch with T.L. not long ago—he was eighty-four years old at the time and had just recently returned from preaching a revival meeting in Paris. More than ten thousand people attended.

After Daisy died, T.L. grieved deeply, but he refused to allow grief to overwhelm him. T.L. has always had an *I must* attitude and he was determined to keep preaching the gospel. He took ownership of his situation: he continued to take care of himself physically and kept on studying and learning new languages. Today, he conducts twelve crusades a year around the world—amazing!

I don't think either T.L. or Daisy set out to change the whole world when they first began their ministry, and I doubt they could have known all God would do through them. But they never underestimated the power of their obedience in the little things. They followed Jesus day by day—going where He led them, doing what He showed them to do, saying what He led them to say and preach and teach. They walked out their faith one faith-filled step at a time.

What a legacy they have as a result! Not only did they directly affect nations for Christ, but God also used this couple to mentor others who would preach the Word around the world. I am humbled to be among those they touched. Years ago, Daisy prophesied over me. She said I would one day speak before the leaders of nations and become known as a world evangelist. At the time, I could scarcely take in what she was saying to me, but I began to pray over her words. Today, Daisy's prophecy is coming to pass: I have traveled to 124 countries and have prayed with many world leaders, including the Ethiopian president, the king of Jordan, and the man who would become prime minister of Israel.

How *exciting* it is to see God work His wonders in each tiny step we take. I feel doubly blessed because, years after Daisy prophesied to me, God called Sarah into the ministry. Today, she and I work side by side to "cover the earth with the Word," and when my work is finished, hers will continue.

Don't Miss Your Golden Opportunity!

Yes, everyone wants to be blessed, but God's vision is long term. He wants *our generations* to be blessed. Consider the example of Abram. Abram's family tree was a mess. He and his forbears lived in pagan Mesopotamia. His family very likely worshiped idols, in a neighborhood that worshiped idols, in a nation that worshiped idols. In fact, one very old Jewish story claims that Terah, Abram's father, made his living by making idols.

So why didn't Abram's family continue to live in pagan obscurity? Very simply because someone obeyed God and became an agent of change. For reasons not stated in the Bible, Terah, Abram's father, uprooted his three sons—Abram, Nahor, and Haran—and their wives, and moved them from Ur of the Chaldees to a place just north of Canaan, which is Israel today. (See Genesis 11:27–32.)

How remarkable for a family in those days to leave the center of their civilization and relocate to a remote area hundreds of miles away. It was a move that literally changed history.

You must realize—and if you absorb this truth it will change your life—God *never* leads His people aimlessly. He always has a direction, a plan, a purpose. He leads us with divine precision and accuracy, and always for good. Psalm 23 speaks of the Shepherd's perfect guidance:

> The LORD is my shepherd;
> I have everything I need.
> He lets me rest in green meadows;
> he leads me beside peaceful streams.
> He renews my strength.
> He guides me along right paths,
> bringing honor to his name.
>
> (PSALM 23:1–3)

Keep your mind and heart tuned to the Great Shepherd's voice and He will *continually* lead you into places of provision, security, restoration, and righteousness. If you continue to follow Him, your family will be *going somewhere* and it will be a place full of God's promise and power.

As was true for Terah, there are times when one of the most important things you can do is to pack up your family and move them to the place God shows you. Be forewarned that reasons to wait or reconsider will immediately spring to mind: *I'll move later, when housing prices are different. I'll move after the school year is over. I'll move if things get worse.* If your reasons to stay are really excuses not to go, then admit it to yourself, repent, and *go!*

Whether God calls you to go or stay, you are God's choice to be *an agent of change*—on your street, in your neighborhood, and in your workplace. God called *you* to be salt and light to the world, a person of influence, an ambassador of the living God, one who carries the message of the King to those around you.

You may be the "Esther" God has chosen in this day to save a people, or the "Abraham" He has appointed to initiate a heritage of righteousness reaching beyond your bloodline and beyond your doorstep. Yes, *you can* do what God asks because His strength is available to you. But if you truly desire what God desires, then the words *I must* will rise up in your spirit and you will be propelled by God's power and might to fulfill your destiny.

Insight from Marilyn

What a great privilege it is for me to count Oral Roberts and his late wife, Evelyn, among my dear friends and colleagues for the gospel.

Evelyn Lutman Roberts was an outstanding woman of faith who was raised in a family that loved God. When she was little, her family moved from Missouri to Kansas *specifically* to learn more about the power of God. Evelyn's stepfather, a man she called "Daddy," heard about a group of people in Coffeyville, Kansas, who were experiencing marvelous things—Evelyn's aunt wrote it was "just like the book of Acts."

Daddy was quick to recognize and respond to an opportunity to improve the lot of his household. He went to Kansas to see what God was doing there and when he returned home, he informed the family they would be locking up the house and moving to Coffeyville.

So off they went! The Lutmans lived there for about a year. Then, when Evelyn was eight years old, Daddy began to scour the countryside looking for a good church and Christian school. Christian schools were rare in the 1920s, but Daddy found one in Checotah, Oklahoma. He moved the family there, determined to provide the ideal setting for the entire family to grow in the faith.

Evelyn's mother was as eager as Daddy to do all she could, so she worked as the housemother of the girls' dorm. Meanwhile, Daddy enrolled in a full-time Bible course while the children studied at the Christian school. When the school closed, Daddy was undaunted; he moved the family to Arkansas and enrolled the children in a new Christian school there.

Evelyn counted her seven years of formal Bible training as a great blessing. It was during those early years she accepted

Jesus as her Savior and Lord and became firmly grounded in her faith. She never wavered from her grounding in the Word of God—she never rebelled against God or the church.

Evelyn wrote in her autobiography, *His Darling Wife, Evelyn,* "I owe much of my spiritual heritage to my stepfather. His remarkable determination to keep the family in a spiritual environment prepared me someday to meet Oral. Although we were poor in material things, we certainly were never impoverished when it came to love or the blessings of God."

Evelyn's stepfather had an *I must* approach to life. His priorities were clear and he did everything in his power to provide his family with an environment that would meet their spiritual needs. Daddy could not see all that would be accomplished through Evelyn's marriage to Oral, but he played a part in their marriage coming to pass. As a result, the world has been profoundly affected by the Roberts family's evangelistic and healing ministry.

Generation blessing is not limited to well-known ministry families. It starts in families like yours. God has a place of destiny for you, a place for your family to be taught the Word of God and experience His presence and power, a place where He desires your family to prosper and bless others. Ask God to reveal that place to you. Then, be quick to obey Him.

Prior to the move by Terah and his family, there is no indication Abram worshiped just one God. It is *after* the move the living God spoke to Abram. We read these five powerful words in Genesis 12:1: "Then the LORD told Abram. . . ."

Abram heard God speak—not a God, *the* God.

Not one of many gods—but the *only* God.

Not a remote cosmic god demanding ritual without relationship—but the *one true* God who desired to be called "Lord," yet longed for intimacy with mortals.

The word "Lord" has to do with relationship—it refers to a benevolent master who takes full responsibility for the provision and protection of an obedient servant. Within the framework of lordship, friendship and love are possible. And that is precisely what happened in the life of Abram. The one true and living God became friends with Abram. (See 2 Chronicles 20:7 and James 2:23.)

Abram moved and in the place where he moved he heard God speak. The Lord's message to Abram was profound:

> *Then the LORD told Abram, "Leave your country, your relatives, and your father's house, and go to the land that I will show you. I will cause you to become the father of a great nation. I will bless you and make you famous, and I will make you a blessing to others. I will bless those who bless you and curse those who curse you. All the families of the earth will be blessed through you." (Genesis 12:1–3)*

The Lord called Abram to move away from his immediate family and go to a specific land God promised to show him. He gave him the outline of his future: great descendants—in fact, a whole nation of them—a great reputation, and great blessing.

What greater future could anyone desire?

A Great Family "Nation"

Every person wants to establish and leave behind a tremendous legacy. Abram, who was seventy-five years old when God gave him this call, did not have any natural children. He was beyond retirement age and the Bible says his body was "as good as dead" (Rom. 4:19 NIV). Yet God promised to make him a great nation.

You may not have any natural, physical children. But in the spirit realm, God always holds out to you this challenge of faith: "I will make of you a great nation." There are no limits on your ability to influence others with the gospel. If you affect just *one person*, God can then use that individual to reach an entire generation. Yes!—in our modern times, you can be the founding ancestor of a great "nation" of godly people.

Pastor Joel Osteen tells a wonderful story about his late father, John Osteen, who founded Lakewood Church. John was a powerful preacher and evangelist, a man who lived to do God's bidding. Years ago, John attended a friend's church. To avoid disturbing others, he sat in a back pew and listened to the sermon. As the service progressed, John noticed a young man sitting across the pew from him. The man looked distraught and John decided to minister to him after the service.

When the service ended, the young man quickly disappeared. John was determined to speak with him, so he searched everywhere, including the lobby and the parking lot, but to no avail.

Then John decided to check the restroom, where he lingered by the sink hoping to spot the young man. Soon the distraught man appeared. John approached him and said, "God loves you, and you are extremely valuable to Him."

Broken, the young man replied, "My life is so messed up. I'm addicted to drugs. I decided I'd come to church one last time and then go home and take every pill I could find."

The enemy's plot was well under way in this man's life, but the obedience of a stranger stopped it cold. This young man had no idea who John Osteen was. He only knew that someone cared enough to reach out to him. John's determination to obey the leading of the Holy Spirit saved the man's life. Thirty years later, the once-distraught young man is the pastor of a church of thousands in Houston, Texas. He has become an agent of change in his community, a leader of a "great nation."

Through his investment in this young man's life, John Osteen left a legacy. It's not his only legacy. John also raised a godly family of his own and a church family that has since become the largest congregation in the United States.

A Great Name

The second part of God's blessing to Abram involved Abram's "name"—his identity, his reputation. The Lord told Abram he would "make thy name great." He would establish Abram's faith as a standard for all generations to come.

It is a powerful legacy to leave behind a great name, one that evokes in the minds of others the memory of one who did good deeds and inspired others to serve God. It is an eternal legacy, one rooted in faith and founded in the relationship between God and man.

Insight from Marilyn

Can a story like Abraham's happen today? Absolutely!

One of the most exciting stories of generational blessing I have ever heard involves the Sewarts, a family ministering in Singapore.

Mrs. Sewart was raised by missionary parents in China. When she was ten years old, the Japanese invaded the area where she and her parents lived and many Americans were raped or killed. Through a series of miraculous circumstances, her family was able to get out of China and return to the

United States, where Mrs. Sewart eventually attended Bible school and married an American.

Together, she and her husband felt a call to pursue missions work in Asia. Unable to go back to China, they went to Singapore, which has a large population of Chinese people. The Sewarts started a church there that is very likely the mother church for all of the great churches in Singapore. Certainly the church has had a major impact on the spiritual life of that entire nation.

Late in her life, Mrs. Sewart was able to return to China. She traveled to the very place her parents had been missionaries and she attended the church they started. An elderly woman in the congregation recognized her—she saw the family resemblance. Mrs. Sewart was able to encourage the people greatly, in part because of her heritage. They saw in her someone who was faithful "from generation to generation"—a child who was carrying on the great name of her parents.

The impact of the Sewart family on Asia spans three generations and their legacy continues to press into the future. All four of the Sewart children are in full-time ministry today, three of them in missions work. One of them leads a large work in Singapore. Their daughter ministers in Nepal, where she has established a Christian work and an orphanage in the face of intense spiritual opposition—she has been thrown in prison often for her strong faith. She is one of the boldest women for Christ I have ever met.

Have the Sewarts encountered problems? Of course. All families do. One of their sons became involved in drugs and alcohol. You can well imagine the heartbreak his family endured and the fervor of their prayers on his behalf. Yet they were faithful to continue their work and, in time, God answered their prayers. Their loved one was miraculously delivered by Jesus Christ—not quietly or privately, but in a very dramatic and public way. This man's encounter with God was so intense, and his deliverance so complete, that today he is involved in missions work in Africa.

Through good times and bad, the Sewarts are blessing a nation, a continent, and the world! Generation after generation.

Blessed . . . to Be a Blessing

Because of what God spoke to him, Abram understood God was going to give him a land, and the land would be fruitful with massive herds and flocks. Abram's God-given wealth was not to be hoarded but shared with other nomadic peoples in the region so Abram might live in peace with his neighbors and the entire population could have its basic needs fully met. But the greater blessing to his neighbors would be Abram's sharing of his faith in God.

As nations came into contact with Abram and were blessed by goods, services, and association with Abram, they would learn about the patriarch's God and begin to follow Him. That was the Lord's plan. It was not a plan of divide and conquer, but rather, a plan of *divide and bless*.

The material prosperity of Abram, the character of Abram, the influence of Abram, and most importantly, the faith of Abram were intended to increase and spread, and to be shared by other peoples, until the whole earth was blessed.

Can you begin to catch a glimpse of the magnificent plan God has in mind for you and your family?

Just look at the way this plan unfolded in the life of Abram.

First, Abram was a great man when he left Haran and began to follow God south into Canaan. Abram did not leave Haran alone. Hundreds of people and thousands of sheep, goats, and cattle also embarked on the journey. But by the end of Abram's life, he was *greatly* increased. Thousands of people were part of his community. He was able to wage war against those who sought to steal from him and win. He had heirs. He had possessions and flocks and herds that gave him the financial means and status to function as an equal with kings and rulers in other territories, including Egypt.

We sometimes think it is strictly an American ideal that parents want more for their children than they themselves had. No! This is God's way and it comes straight from the Bible. God's plan is for increase through the generations. God desires for your children to excel to greater heights, to experience greater blessings, to achieve more and give more than you were able to achieve or give.

Second, Abram's identity was changed. God did this with a change of name, which is often the way God dealt with people in Bible times. Fifteen years after Abram left Haran and made his way into Canaan, the Lord spoke to Abram and said:

> *"I am God Almighty; walk before me and be blameless. I will confirm my covenant between me and you and will greatly increase your numbers."*
>
> *Abram fell facedown, and God said to him, "As for me, this is my covenant with you: You will be the father of many nations. No longer will you be called Abram; your name will be Abraham, for I have made you a father of many nations. I will make you very fruitful; I will make nations of you, and kings will come from you. I will establish my covenant as an everlasting covenant between me and you and your descendants after you for the generations to come, to be your God and the God of your descendants after you. The whole land of Canaan, where you are now an alien, I will give as an everlasting possession to you and your descendants after you; and I will be their God." (Genesis 17:1–8 NIV)*

Abram was a name meaning "an exalted father." Abram was a name that referred to the character quality of Abram's life. Even though he was not yet a father to a son in the physical realm, he was a leader of others who thought of him in fatherly terms. Abram had the nature of a father.

In contrast, *Abraham* was a name that meant "father of a multitude." This name indicated increase. God gave him a new name in part because He was extending Abraham's role as a leader far beyond his known relatives. It is an expansive name, a name elevating Abraham to a new level of influence and wealth.

Note what God commanded Abraham: "Walk before me, and be blameless" (Gen. 17:1 NIV). This word *blameless* doesn't mean without fault, but rather, without wavering or detouring. It refers to walking faithfully, steadfastly, and with singular focus. It means Abraham was to listen intently to *every* word God spoke and to embrace every word *fully* and *immediately*.

That is the essence of obedience, the heart of an *I must* attitude toward life. And the obedience of Abraham would be greatly rewarded with:

• *Exceeding fruitfulness*. Abraham's life was multiplied. His fruitfulness extends throughout the world. His influence has spread horizontally, across the planet.

• *A heritage of faithful heirs*. Abraham's heirs are as uncountable as the grains of sand on the seashore. His fruitfulness has extended through time, not just space. His legacy is generational, spanning world history since his day.

• *A lasting and unbroken possession*. The land would belong to his heirs *permanently*. The land of Abraham became the land of Isaac, which became the land of Jacob (renamed *Israel* by God), which became the land of the twelve tribes of Israel, which continues today as the nation of Israel.

The rewards promised to Abraham are the same rewards God holds out to you as you live a righteous, faith-filled *life of obedience*:

- *Fruitfulness*—a life and legacy of increase, influence, and effectiveness in the earth for you and your heirs.
- *A heritage of natural and spiritual heirs*—your physical children (adopted and biological) and your spiritual children, entrusted to you by God, who will spread your legacy of fruitfulness over space and time.
- *A supernatural place of provision and protection*—the place or places to which God will lead you to establish and benefit you and your family, the place where He will cause you to influence others for His glory.

Insight from Marilyn

Earlier, I mentioned T. L. Osborn's recent crusade in Paris. When I visited with T.L. at his home, he showed me a panoramic photo of the thousands who attended the Paris meeting.

I was astounded to see such crowds, because I know how secular, and even atheistic, much of France is today. As I gazed at the photo, I noticed many of the people pictured were Africans. My curiosity increased and I asked T.L., "How did you draw such a large crowd in France, and how is it that so many Africans attended your Paris meeting?"

T.L. smiled and shared the testimony that began decades before. He explained that early in his and Daisy's ministry, God prompted the couple to hold meetings in France. They were certain they heard from God, so they arranged to minister there.

In spite of their obedience, the meetings seemed to be an utter failure. Attendance was low and the results disappointing. After a string of failed meetings, T.L. asked God, "Why do You ask us to preach there if the ministry continues to be fruitless?"

Finally, God said, "I have one more idea for you. I want you to go to the French-speaking nations in Africa and preach the gospel there."

T.L. and Daisy obeyed, arranging meetings in several countries. The meetings were tremendously successful and churches were birthed as a result.

Decades later, many French-speaking Africans, including the descendants of those who attended the Osborns' early meetings on "the dark continent," migrated to France. In 2006, when God called T.L. to hold a crusade in Paris, guess who financed the meeting? Yes! The African-Christian community, those whose parents and grandparents in the homeland had come to Christ under the ministry of T. L. and Daisy Osborn.

Through the Osborns' dogged obedience and the perseverance of a godly generation, a *new generation* was reached with the gospel, and in a nation where ministry seemed fruitless so many years before, seeds of faith are now planted in a softening ground, ripe for revival.

Yes, *your* obedience will leave a legacy, a legacy of fruitfulness, a heritage of faithful heirs, and a lasting and unbroken possession for God's glory! Act on His promises and teach your children to do the same. Fulfill His mandates. Claim the rewards of obedience for your family lineage, and you will create a heavenly deposit box of benefits—a reserve of rewards from heaven—for generations to come.

DIVINE INTERRUPTION

*B*e purposeful in asking the Lord where the best place might be for you to live or to raise a family. You might be right where you need to be, but if He shows you someplace unexpected, don't worry. If He sends you, He will send the blessings, too, and your obedience will be rewarded.

8

Get Under the Downspout of Blessing

What would you say if a roving reporter stopped you on the street and asked, "Do *you* want to be blessed?"

Would you have to pause, collect your thoughts, and weigh the pros and cons before responding? No! Your reply, and everyone else's, would be a resounding "Yes!" But if the reporter asked a dozen people what it *means* to be blessed, twelve unique answers would result.

Each of us has a distinct mental picture of what blessing looks like. Yet, there are certain characteristics that speak of blessing to just about everyone: sufficient health and energy, enough money, loving family relationships and friends, a good church, a long life, a nation in which we can exercise freedom of speech, freedom of assembly, and freedom of religion. Simply put, we define "the good life" as a blessed life.

People in other nations often measure blessing by very different standards. In some places, you are considered extremely blessed if you have enough to eat in a given day or if your newborn baby survives more than a few days. In regions where religious persecution is common, being blessed means not being imprisoned for your faith.

Regardless of our individual experiences, believers can agree that blessing is *an act of God's goodness*:

• *A blessing cannot exist apart from God.* Blessing is not something we can produce on our own, create out of our own ingenuity, or earn with our own effort. A blessing is a gift of God. Even when we think we have achieved a blessing, if we are truly honest with ourselves, we must admit we only played a part in bringing the blessing about. It is God who gives us every breath we breathe, every ounce of energy and strength we have, every beat of our heart, every fresh and pure idea, every minute of life, and every opportunity.

• *A blessing expresses the character of God.* We receive as blessings those things that exemplify God, things we perceive to be fruitful, beneficial, positive, and helpful. When we are blessed, we respond in God-like ways by blessing others. In this way, blessing reaches beyond the realm of the finite.

We know from Scripture that the opposite of a blessing is a curse. Malachi, the last great prophet in Israel, who lived nearly four hundred years before John the Baptist, rebuked God's people and warned them against forfeiting God's blessing and coming under a curse.

Israel's "right living" became watered down. The people were going through the motions of worship, but their "doing" was no longer motivated by a desire to please God. They spoke against the temple worship, saying, "It's too hard to serve the LORD." (Mal. 1:13). The priests in the temple were offering "polluted bread" on the table of showbread, and they were offering blind, lame, and sick animals as burnt sacrifices, in direct disobedience to the Law of Moses. This was regarded by God as contempt—not only contempt for the Law, but contempt for God.

God was not only concerned with the *behaviors* of His people and His priests, but with the general pervasive *attitude* the people had toward God and His commandments. God warned that judgment would result: "'Listen to me and take it to heart. Honor my name,' says the LORD Almighty, "'or I will bring a terrible curse against you. I will curse even the blessings you receive'" (Mal. 2:2).

These are some of the strongest words of rebuke found in the Bible. Through Malachi, God brought correction and a reminder of the blessings the people were in danger of losing:

> "*The purpose of my covenant with the Levites was to bring life and peace, and this is what I gave them. This called for reverence from them, and they greatly revered me and stood in awe of my name. They passed on to the people all the truth they received from me. They did not lie or cheat; they walked with me, living good and righteous lives, and they turned many from lives of sin. The priests' lips should guard knowledge, and people should go to them for instruction, for the priests are the messengers of the LORD Almighty. But not you! You have left God's paths. Your 'guidance' has caused many to stumble into sin. You have corrupted the covenant I made with the Levites,*" says the LORD Almighty. (Malachi 2:5–8)

As a good Father, God sometimes administers tough love in order to protect His people. The Bible records these examples of strong rebuke and does not underplay those occasions when God's words are stern and matter-of-fact.

However, the Bible also proclaims the sweet and wonderful benefits accruing for those who choose God's ways. We will call these benefits *hallmarks of blessing*. Over the coming chapters, we will focus on eight facets of God's blessing to us and our loved ones. These hallmarks present a rich, well-rounded picture of what it means to be blessed.

Hallmark of Blessing #1:
The Vibrant Life of a Blessed Generation

To experience a vibrant life, we must first realize all blessing is first and foremost *spiritual* in nature. Our spiritual life is largely internal. Righteousness, truth, faith, and obedience begin on the inside of us and when we choose to walk in them, we begin to live supernaturally. In this way, the internal spiritual life is manifested externally. The psalmist said it this way: "Happy are those who fear the LORD. Yes, happy are those who delight in doing what he commands. Their children will be successful everywhere; an entire generation of godly people will be blessed" (Ps. 112:1–2).

Remember that Malachi's warning was to those who no longer feared God. The psalmist, on the other hand, explains the fear of God leads to happiness, success, and blessing. In other words, those who delight in God's commands *position* themselves and their children under the downspout of blessing.

Insight from Marilyn

A friend once shared with me wonderful words of wisdom she received from her godly grandmother many years before. Granny, as my friend called her, lived on a farm at the outskirts of the town where my friend grew up. My friend often rode her bicycle out to visit Granny and Pawpaw. She said one of her favorite things to do was to draw well water from a pump on the little farm. The water was sweet, pure, and very cold. She had a little pail all her own she kept at Granny's house—her name was brightly painted on its side: Linda.

One day Linda was being a little careless in the way she pumped water into her pail. She was so preoccupied with handling the lever of the pump she failed to notice the water splashing on the ground at the side of her container, rather than filling it. Granny laughed and pointed out what was happening, and after the pail was repositioned and a full pail of water carried to the back porch, Granny and Linda sat on the porch swing and Granny made this profound statement. "What you just experienced is a picture of the way God wants to bless us."

"It is?" Linda said.

"Yes," said Granny. "God has unlimited blessings for you, Linda. His blessings are like the water that comes up from the well—they are sweet and pure and refreshing. The pump is your faith and work combined. When you pump the lever, you *expect* water to come up, and it does. But it also takes effort to move that lever. God honors our faith when we put our faith into action."

"What about the pail?" inquired Linda.

"The pail," Granny explained, "is your life. God wants to fill you up to the brim and overflowing, so you have the blessings of God to quench the thirst in your life and also to give to others what will quench the thirst in their lives. Thirst, of course, is far more than your physical thirst for water. It can be their thirst for knowledge of the things of God, for health, for salvation. Whatever God pours into you, He expects you to give out to others."

Linda told me they sat swinging for a few moments and then Granny added one more thing.

"None of this works the way God designed it to work, however, if your pail isn't in right position," Granny said with a smile.

"I know," Linda said. "The pail has to be under the pipe where the water comes out."

"Being in position is critically important," Granny said. "To be blessed, you have to be in the right position. You have to be in obedience to God. You have to be looking up to Him to fill you."

Linda said to me as she told me this story, "I've never forgotten those words of my grandmother. God has such tremendous blessings for each one of us who love Him. We need to stay in the right position to receive them. We need to stay under the downspout!"

Being in position to receive from God is directly tied to worshiping Him. The Bible says we are each called to worship God *in spirit and in truth*. In other words, we worship God *in our hearts* (spirit) and *in our actions* (truth). We are called to love God with our hearts, minds, souls, and strength. We do this by giving thanks and praise to God. We are also called to love our neighbors as ourselves. We can do this in practical, real-world ways.

Two Big Es

You have two kinds of neighbors, those who believe in Christ and those who don't. Either way, we are called to love our neighbors in ways that build the kingdom and build up others. We'll call these good works *The Big Es*. Let's start by discussing simple ways by which we can build the kingdom.

1. Expand *God's Kingdom by Reaching the Lost.*
In the simplest terms, we are called to expand the kingdom by sharing the message of the gospel—the good news of Christ—with the unbeliever.

This simply means sharing our faith with others, by whatever method is suitable in a given situation. You might feel called to go door-to-door in your neighborhood or to pass out tracts on the street. However, expanding the kingdom can be as simple as hosting a Bible study in your home and inviting your neighbors, mentioning the name of Jesus in a conversation, or sharing the story of how you came to have faith in Christ. You can expand the kingdom just by answering the questions of those who wonder why you trust God the way you do. These acts of sharing the good news of Jesus with other people are "seeds" God can use to change lives.

The Bible says God confirms what we say and do in reaching the unbeliever with miracles, signs, and wonders. (See Hebrews 2:3–4 and Acts 2:43, 15:12.) In other words, God supernaturally backs up our outreach with supernatural acts that cement the truth we have shared in the minds of those to whom we minister.

Insight from Marilyn

God's signs and wonders aren't always spectacular events visible to the natural eye. One of our ministry employees—we'll call her Rosemarie—recently shared about the supernatural way in which God "spoke" to her unsaved friend, a man we'll call Scott.

Scott and Rosemarie had known each other for decades, but hadn't seen one another in sixteen years. One night, the two had a lengthy conversation, catching up on all that was going on in their lives. It was a lively discussion, not religious really, but sprinkled with spiritual overtones. Although Scott does not profess to be a Christian, he believes in God and is comfortable talking about Him.

When Rosemarie suggested Scott check out our church service the following night, he resisted. However, by the next day he agreed to attend. Scott didn't know quite what to expect but found the "church people" were friendly and made him feel at home.

Within minutes of the start of the sermon, God performed signs and wonders specifically aimed at Scott's heart. Woven into the teaching were all the ideas and issues that Scott and Rosemarie discussed the night before, along with answers to some of the questions raised during their conversation.

Scott began to poke his elbow into Rosemarie's ribs, saying, "Did you hear that? How can this be? How could anyone else know about the things we talked about? Our entire conversation is being repeated in this sermon!"

God revealed Himself to Scott in a very personal way. Scott *enjoyed* church and understood that something supernatural—what the Bible calls signs and wonders—had occurred.

What happens next is up to God and Scott, but good spiritual seed was sown, and it *will* bear fruit in its time.

2. Enrich *the Lives of Our Fellow Believers by Encouraging Them.*

Another form of personal outreach is to encourage fellow believers. When we encourage Christians, we build up or add value to them. In this way, their faith is strengthened and their relationship with God deepens. Often, we give obvious spiritual support by sharing a Scripture or praying, but sometimes we help our fellow Christians by simply being there for them in difficult times. We can also encourage others by applauding their achievements or writing little notes to say, "You are a blessing to me."

What we do in building the kingdom and building up our fellow believers comes back to us. Why? Because both involve acts of giving, and giving always comes back around in God's economy.

Insight from Marilyn

To many Christians, reaching out to the unsaved or even encouraging the believer can be intimidating. We can become overly fearful that, if we talk about God, we will offend others. Rather than worry about offending, focus on the blessing you can release into another person's life. Chances are *your life* was changed when people shared the gospel or encouraged you—and aren't you glad they did?

My husband, Wally, and I love to hold what we call "*sinners' dinners.*" We invite neighbors and acquaintances to our home on a regular basis. Recently, we invited three young women who run the salon where I have my nails done. They are Vietnamese Buddhists, not very religious, but fun-loving people enjoying the American lifestyle.

The first time I visited their salon, I noticed some Buddhist religious symbols there. We chatted away, exchanging questions. I learned they all really loved chocolates and they learned I was a Christian. They had never been to a Christian church, so I invited them.

They had questions about what they heard at church, so we began to have little Bible studies. From time to time, I brought them gifts of their favorite chocolates. On the night of our special dinner together, they came with their boyfriends and prepared a fabulous Vietnamese meal. You can imagine the setting: they took over our kitchen and filled our home with laughter. We dined together and enjoyed spirited conversation.

In this relaxed atmosphere, it was easy to talk more about Christ. One of these young gals has given her life to the Lord and I encourage her faith (or *edify* her)—every chance I get. Still, we're believing for all three, and their boyfriends, to get saved.

That isn't all we're praying for. There are twenty thousand Vietnamese living in our city. We are asking God to use these three young women to reach their community and, in time, for a Vietnamese church to be established. I've already told the one gal I know is saved that she needn't count on us to preach at the Vietnamese church, because God can use *her* to evangelize her community. She responded excitedly, "I had better get off my butt and get in my Bible!"

God has written these women on my heart, therefore, *I must* continue to reach out to them. (See 2 Corinthians 3:2–3.) I know that, little by little, the spiritual seed Wally and I are planting is taking root. When we started our Bible studies with these women, I would always close in prayer. Now, as we near the end of a study, they're quick to say, "We need to pray!" This is exactly how generational blessing can begin: one soul, or three souls, at a time.

With whom can you share the gospel, and whom can you encourage today? Ask the Lord to show you how to reach out to others. What we give to others—even chocolates—can be used by God to open a conversation about Christ.

YOU CAN'T OUTGIVE GOD

When we share our faith, we are *giving* the gospel to another person or a group of people. When we share our material blessings and spiritual gifts, we are *giving* to meet a need or to complete the ministry of the Lord in another person's life. Jesus' promise is that whatever we *give* is multiplied by God and returned to us as a blessing far greater than what we gave. Jesus said: "If you give, you will receive. Your gift will return to you in full measure, pressed down, shaken together to make room for more, and running over. Whatever measure you use in giving—large or small—it will be used to measure what is given back to you" (Luke 6:38).

We sometimes limit this verse in the church to refer only to the giving and receiving of money or material goods. In truth, Jesus was referring to all acts that flow from a generous heart:

- If you give of your time to the church or to those who need your help, your giving will return to you, perhaps in the form of increased productivity in your own endeavors.
- If you are a loving person, always friendly and quick to encourage others, you will receive more love than you gave out.
- If you are diligent and always do your best for your employer, you will receive favor and promotion in return.
- If you pour guidance, wisdom, and love into your children, you will receive the wonder of watching them develop and grow strong, do good works, and raise healthy families of their own. You will also receive from them honor in the years to come.

Perhaps the most fundamental area of financial giving is the paying of the tithe. Remember that we are to worship God in spirit and in truth. Faithfulness in tithing demonstrates a heart of worship, the acknowledgment that all we have comes from God.

Malachi describes the profound benefits of tithing.

> *"Bring all the tithes into the storehouse so there will be enough food in my Temple. If you do,"* says the LORD Almighty, *"I will open the windows of heaven for you. I will pour out a blessing so great you won't have enough room to take it in! Try it! Let me prove it to you!" (Malachi 3:10)*

Whether in tithes, offerings, the giving of one's time, or in volunteering to help others, a person simply cannot outgive God. Whatever we give in His name and to accomplish His work sets in motion a cycle resulting in our *receiving* what we need in our lives, *and more!* Everything we receive from the hand of God is fully sufficient, *pressed down and shaken together,* and with much left over. The *running-over* aspect of our blessing is given to us so we might share with others.

Note that sentence in Jesus' teaching: "Whatever measure you use in giving . . . it will be used to measure what is given back to you" (Luke 6:38). If you give in teaspoon-size doses, you'll receive in like manner. If you truly want to be in the full flow of God's giving and receiving, give *generously.* God loves a generous heart.

Insight from Sarah

Mom tells the story of how she began to tithe when she was eleven years old. It was one of the principles my grandmother sowed into our family.

When Mom went to college in Greeley, Colorado, she paid her own way—every bit of it. Winters can be pretty tough there, so Mom wore a fur coat to keep warm. Fur may have been popular in those days, but it was expensive. Not surprisingly, Mom was the only one on campus wearing a fur coat. And she graduated college completely debt-free, one of very few who left school without a loan to repay.

Our family's heritage of tithing is a generational blessing. In God's plan, each generation should be more blessed than the one before. I can see that in the area of giving: Mom began tithing at age eleven, but I was just six when I started. In fact, I took it a step further by tithing, not on the amount of allowance I received each week, but on the amount I was believing for. Sounds almost entrepreneurial—and it was—but it was first and foremost a matter of faith.

My children are age six and under, but they've been involved in giving for a long time. My parents or my husband and I would often give them money specifically for the offering. They learned about giving in a hands-on way. Now, apart from their own giving, they love being entrusted to place Mom and Dad's tithe into the bucket as it moves down the row.

My children are not only benefiting from what our family has learned over the generations, they have become part of the "blessing chain" and are light-years ahead of Reece and me at their ages. Unless Jesus comes first, they will continue the process by passing the same blessings, and new ones, forward to their own children.

What are the gifts, spiritual and otherwise, God has given you? Whatever they are—talents, time, inspired words, a cheerful heart—be quick to share them. The more you give, the greater your own joy and feelings of fulfillment. As you give, you will develop an increased expectancy about all God might do *in your life*, and *through your life* to others.

How does this relate to establishing generational blessings in your family? It's as simple as it is profound: teach your children to share their spiritual gifts within the family first. Model the practice of giving by your example. Be generous toward your family members. Study the spiritual gifts described in Romans 12 and 1 Corinthians 12 and assess which ones seem to be most prominent in your life. Help your children discover the gifts that are prominent in their lives, then help them to find ways to use those gifts to bless other members of the family and to sharpen their own God-given abilities.

Highlight the benefits of encouraging others. Your children will quickly learn they have everything to gain and nothing to lose by applauding the successes of their siblings. When you attend your children's games and performances, applaud their successes and comfort them in their failures. Be your children's biggest fan. Doing so will produce children who are well adjusted and secure and who find it easy to root for others.

Just as affirmation builds up your children, overlooking your children's accomplishments or focusing only on their shortcomings will lead to hopelessness in the short term and hardness of heart over time.

Insight from Sarah

Recently I read a tragic story about a middle-aged man who put a shotgun to his head on a cold December day and pulled the trigger.

I tell this story to illustrate the damage that can be done when children do not receive encouragement from their parents or are abused by those entrusted to care for them. We'll call the man Tim.

It was Christmastime and the holiday season was in full swing. Stores were bustling, homes were bedecked in shimmering lights, and Christmas carols were playing. But, in the midst of the gaiety, Tim's heart was breaking. As he had for years, Tim watched a classic Christmas film. The film should have lifted his spirits, but it only served to make him more depressed. The next day, Tim would commit suicide. The movie—and everything related to Christmas—reminded Tim of his dad's cruelty toward Tim and his brothers.

Each year at Christmastime, the boys worked hard on the family farm. Their dad treated them harshly: he criticized their work, demeaned them terribly, and even beat them to the point that blood would trickle onto their clothing.

Every December, instead of hearing heartwarming stories of love and forgiveness as other children did, Tim and his brothers suffered physical and emotional abuse at the hands of their father. Tim feared his dad and hated him more with each passing year. And because he never forgave his dad, Tim never experienced a healed heart. In fact, each year, his heart grew harder. He hated Christmas and swore that, if he ever killed himself, it would be at Christmastime.

That is exactly what Tim did. He watched the holiday film

one last time. As he did, the painful memories came alive again. Tim sank deeper into discouragement and depression than he ever had before—deep enough to make the dark decision to end his life.

Decades before, Tim's dad failed to see that the seeds of anger, resentment, despair, and depression he was planting in his son's heart would deliver a deadly harvest. Somehow, he missed the opportunity—as we all do at times, to encourage someone he loved.

This story reminds me how deliberate we must be in establishing generation blessing in our families. It doesn't happen by default or by accident; it takes a proactive approach to doing things God's way: loving our kids, taking time to build them up emotionally and spiritually, and sacrificing to give them a leg up in life.

Tim's story is heartbreaking. Yet, there is good news. Even if you were raised by a father like Tim's, and even if you've made mistakes raising your own children, it's never too late to establish a pattern of generation blessing. Simply make a decision to turn around and follow God's ways from here on out. You won't do everything right; who could? But even one person can turn the tide and transform his or her family's future.

Family Choices You Can Make . . . Now

You are the one who determines the spiritual tone in your home, as well as the practical dynamics of your family. Take charge! Choose to become a family that enjoys the full blessings of a vibrant life—spiritually and in every way.

Although change takes time and the effects of your choices will add up over the long term, don't be surprised to see encouraging results in the here and now.

1. Be Your Child's Biggest Fan.

Take the time to let your children experience your love in meaningful ways. Praise their accomplishments and show them the respect due God's children by valuing their thoughts and ideas. When they're discouraged, be the safe haven in which they can discuss their fears, disappointments, and weaknesses.

2. Set the Spiritual Tone for Your Family.

Establish times to pray with your children. Take them to church with you, even when they complain about it. Many so-called experts believe forcing your children to go to church violates their right to choose. In reality, your children depend on you for guidance in making good choices. And if you don't influence your children's decisions in their formative years, *who will?*

3. Find Healthy Social Outlets for Your Children.

Get your children involved in Christ-centered activities, including Sunday school and youth programs. Be enthusiastic when you present these opportunities to your child; he or she will appreciate your input and realize you have their best interests at heart.

4. Help Your Children Develop Hearts to Help Others.

Encourage your children to become involved in age-appropriate ministry opportunities. Help them raise funds to go on a mission trip. Get them involved in a community outreach project at church. Choose together what you might do *as a family* to bless your church or your community.

Many families in our church are reaping the generational blessings resulting from a lifetime of sowing into the lives of others. On a recent mission to China and Cambodia, we worked alongside Aaron and Tyler, two exuberant young men from families that have served selflessly in our church for many years.

For both men, the mission to Asia was a dream come true. They are passionate about the things of God and about reaching the lost; they are excited about the things they are able to do for God. Yet, Aaron and Tyler take no credit for the work they did in China or Cambodia. They believe the opportunity to serve in Asia was a blessing they reaped without sowing.

Aaron and Tyler are convinced their mission trip is a direct result of what their parents have sown into their lives and into the church over the years. Because their parents kept them in church, they learned God's Word and received sound mentoring from youth leaders throughout their lifetimes. This strong spiritual rearing strengthened their love of God. Watching their parents' commitment to serve others, they learned the value of a life of service. And because they "bloomed where they were planted," they were right where they needed to be to participate in the Asia mission. In other words, Aaron and Tyler were perfectly positioned under the downspout of blessing.

How far-reaching are the results of their experiences? It's impossible to quantify. But if you ask them, Aaron and Tyler will tell you they planted every spiritual seed they could in China and Cambodia. They realize they were given the opportunity to take the outflow of the generation blessing operating in their own lives and lay the groundwork for a pattern of generation blessing in places where, for many, blessing is nowhere to be found.

Aaron and Tyler took great risks to evangelize in Asia. Yet, they don't talk about the danger; they share excitedly about the results, the potential, and God's glory being manifested wherever they went. Their reward? Hearing God's voice when their work is done, saying, "Well done, good and faithful servant!"

When you position your children for blessing, their reward is yours too. You and your family were designed by God to leave an imprint on the world. That is *extreme* generation blessing.

POWER POINT

God has given each of us a "pail" He desires to fill with His blessings. If we will ask Him, God will show us exactly where the downspout of our blessing is—and He will show us how to position our "pail" to receive it!

9

Sow Supernatural Seed and Reap a Generational Harvest

❧

Cambodians tell the story of the first Christian missionary who arrived in the predominantly Buddhist nation in 1923. The missionary worked hard, with little success; spiritually speaking, the ground was hard and unresponsive. Still, the missionary continued his work to spread the gospel. In time, his labor began to yield fruit and he was able to plant churches. These churches not only grew in size, but they multiplied over the years.

However, in May 1976, one of the most brutal dictators of all time, Pol Pot, came to power. Cambodia entered a period of utter darkness. Under Pol Pot's evil hand, the nation became a killing field where millions of innocent people from all walks of life perished.

Whereas the lone missionary came to Cambodia to plant seeds of joy and peace, Pol Pot cultivated a harvest of death and destruction. The slaughter brought Cambodia to her knees. Terror paralyzed the nation. Unknown numbers of Christians were among the dead. While the bloodletting drove the church underground, and the missionary's seeds of righteousness seemed to lay dormant, the spiritual soil he tilled would produce again.

Fast forward to the twenty-first century. Due to the genocide, 80 percent of Cambodians are under the age of thirty. This youthful nation—so long laden with horror and heartbreak—is in the midst of *revival*! During our 2006 mission there, the spiritual shift was apparent—hundreds of Christian pastors and leaders attended our ministry training school, more than sixteen thousand flocked to our healing meetings and many were miraculously healed, and Cambodia held its first-ever Christian Fair—outdoors.

We were given the marvelous opportunity to water the ground tilled by God's servant eighty years earlier. His labor was not in vain. Notwithstanding the overwhelming force of Pol Pot and the Khmer Rouge, the devil's attempts to eradicate the church failed, because there was *life* tucked into every seed the missionary planted. By the grace of God and the sweat of his brow, he set in motion a heritage of blessing for a nation *and* her generations.

That is one of the qualities of generation blessing: it cannot be confined by time and space or stamped out by circumstances. It does not deal in *sufficiency*, but in *overflow,* to another person, another generation, another culture, another place and time.

The incredible realm of blessing lies beyond the basics of sufficiency. The second hallmark of blessing deals with having more than enough. But first, let's talk about the mechanics of the seed, which is where every blessing begins.

The Essentials of Seed Power

We have talked about seed in previous chapters, but let's examine seven distinct properties of seeds more closely.

1. Seeds Are God's Building Blocks.

In the beginning, God spoke about seed. When He set the worlds in motion, he tucked seeds inside each of the life forms He created. This seed would ensure that life would spread and continue. "Then God said, 'Let the land burst forth with every sort of grass and seed-bearing plant. And let there be trees that grow seed-bearing fruit. The seeds will then produce the kinds of plants and trees from which they came.' And so it was." (Gen. 1:11).

2. Seeds Have the Potential to Multiply.

Seeds produce multiplication. A single seed births one plant, which potentially bears multiple fruits. Each fruit contains seed of its own—in many cases, numerous seeds. Therefore, certain plants have the potential to produce hundreds of seeds—each capable of producing a new plant.

Genesis 1:12 says that seed accomplished precisely what God planned: "The land was filled with seed-bearing plants and trees, and their seeds produced plants and trees of like kind." This multiplication was not just for plant life; God expected increase from His creatures, too: "So God created great sea creatures and every sort of fish and every kind of bird. And God saw that it was good. Then God blessed them, saying, 'Let the fish multiply and fill the oceans. Let the birds increase and fill the earth.'" (Gen. 1:21–22).

3. Seeds Are God's Plan for Provision.

God created seed with provision in mind. The nourishment of man and the animal kingdom would be provided through seed. "And God said, 'Look! I have given you the seed-bearing plants throughout the earth and all the fruit trees for your food. And I have given all the grasses and other green plants to the animals and birds for their food.' And so it was" (Gen. 1:29–30).

4. The Harvest Involves God and Man.

God provides the seed, but a person plants the seed and cultivates the growth. Then the seed will be fully productive. "When the LORD God made the heavens and the earth, there were no plants or grain growing on the earth, for the LORD God had not sent any rain. And no one was there to cultivate the soil" (Gen. 2:4–5).

5. Seedtime and Harvest Will Never Cease.

Just as night and day continue and the seasons march on, the cycle of seedtime and harvest is ongoing. Ideally, we will always be sowing and, therefore, always reaping. "As long as the earth remains, there will be springtime and harvest, cold and heat, winter and summer, day and night" (Gen. 8:22).

6. The Curse of Sin Corrupts the Seed Growing Process.

Ever since the Fall of Man, harvest can occur only through toil and resistance to opposition. Successful seed-growing requires persistence on the part of the grower.

> Then he said to the woman, "You will bear children with intense pain and suffering. And though your desire will be for your husband, he will be your master." And to Adam he said, "Because you listened to your wife and ate the fruit I told you not to eat, I have placed a curse on the ground. All your life you will struggle to scratch a living from it. It will grow thorns and thistles for you,

though you will eat of its grains. All your life you will sweat to produce food, until your dying day." (Genesis 3:16–19)

7. God's Plan for Redemption Was a "Seed."

The sin of Adam and Eve brought the curse upon the earth. God answered the world's greatest problem, with a seed, His Son. "And I will put enmity between you and the woman, and between your seed and her Seed; he shall bruise your head, and you shall bruise His heel" (Gen. 3:15 NKJV).

The answer to every challenge we face is found in a seed. How we handle the seed we are given will determine the level of our harvest; will we reap barely enough or experience overflowing abundance?

Hallmark of Blessing #2:
God's Abundance — Overflowing Quantity

In Matthew 25, Jesus tells us how to live in abundance: we are to take everything He has given us and maximize its potential by putting it to work for good. He promises, "To those who use well what they are given, even more will be given, and they will have an abundance" (Matt. 25:29).

Paul explains abundance more specifically in terms of sowing and reaping, giving and receiving:

Remember this: Whoever sows sparingly will also reap sparingly, and whoever sows generously will also reap generously. Each man should give what he has decided in his heart to give, not reluctantly or under compulsion, for God loves a cheerful giver. And God is able to make all grace abound to you, so that in all things at all times,

*having all that you need, you will abound in every good
work. (2 Corinthians 9:6–8 NIV)*

Can you see how the power of blessing operates? Cheerful
giving produces harvest, meets needs, generates grace, and increases our ability to perform good works. Imagine how your
quality of life and the quality of your family life are transformed when "*all* grace is abounding to you"!

AN INCREASING CAPACITY TO RECEIVE

God's principles of giving and receiving, essentially, sowing
and reaping, are irrefutable: the more you give, the more you
receive, including greater and greater opportunities, a greater
capacity to earn, produce, work, minister, create, problem-
solve, and communicate with others.

Insight from Sarah

Reece and I have noticed how our children are able to do more
and learn more than we did at their ages. That's true in the
areas of giving and receiving, but it's also the case in many
other areas. That's not unique to our family—it's just the way
generation blessing works. Each generation exceeds the one
before.

For instance, I knew how to count to ten long before I
went to school. My children know how to count to ten in En-
glish and Mandarin, and we are working on Spanish. I knew
Bible verses by memory. My children are memorizing Bible
passages.

Are kids smarter these days? Maybe. But I'm sure of this:

as each generation exceeds the one before, the level of expectation for the *next* generation goes up—and children rise to the level of our expectations.

Raising the level of our expectations in healthy ways can lead to improved performance and a better quality of life. It is a well-known fact that none of us uses all of our capacity in any area of life. Those who have studied the mind say the most brilliant and creative people use less than 10 percent of their mental capacity. Just think what lies in the realm of the unused portion of our ability to think, create, or problem solve.

God asks us to use well what we have been given. How can we apply that command to our unused brainpower? Simple. We can increase our mental capacity by focusing our thoughts and applying valuable information to practical needs. Useful information in; applied wisdom out. It's a giving and receiving process that will produce *more* brainpower.

The same is true for physical fitness. If you study the statistics, the vast majority of people in our nation today are only about 20 percent fit. That adds up to an awful lot of undeveloped physical capacity. As a nation we are underproducing because our bodies are not as well tuned as they could be.

How can we put our physical bodies to better use? We can become more fit through better nutrition, adequate rest, and appropriate exercise. Again, it's a giving and receiving process by which we can put to better use that which we have been given and thereby receive more.

The process by which we grow *spiritually* fit is the same: as we take in more and more of God's Word and God's love, we are able to give out more of God's Word and God's presence. As we do this, God promises we will receive more in return. It's giving and receiving, sowing and reaping, seedtime and harvest. It is the way abundance happens.

AN EXPANDING DESIRE TO GIVE

"It is more blessed to give than to receive." It is the nature of God and His economy that we experience abundance and fulfillment, not by receiving, but by giving. If we are enriched by giving, what will *more giving* do? Another aspect of the seed principle is this: as you give, your desire to give increases.

You may find yourself sowing financial seed into a wider range of needs. Or you might burrow deeper into a specific need as God leads. In either case, God will cause your giving to be fully productive. While God uses your seed to meet the needs of others, He will cause the generosity of others to meet *your* need. (See Luke 6:38.)

Through your involvement in helping others, God may reveal more of His vision for your life. For example, as you become involved in giving to a specific cause—feeding the homeless, providing disaster relief, or visiting the sick—you may discover a growing desire to help. Don't be surprised if you are presented with opportunities to apply your skills to a greater degree. God will further develop your gifts and talents for kingdom use *and* for your personal growth.

When God is involved, one seed can produce many harvests. We see this principle at work in nature. A single tree will drop many acorns. One acorn becomes food for a squirrel and because the squirrel is well fed, he is productive. He produces offspring, and his generations continue to reproduce.

Another acorn may take root and produce a tree that will produce many more acorns over time. In this way, the continuance of the species and its role in nature are ensured.

Many other harvests are possible. One tree might be used to frame someone's home or furnish a classroom, while another tree is processed to produce paper—perhaps tracts that will be distributed in China, where each tract delivers the gospel to five people, who in turn will share the gospel with others.

God's economy is brilliant—and we are part of it!

Insight from Marilyn

Years ago, I had a great desire to win my neighborhood for Christ. I knew the entire world needed to know about Jesus, but I believed my role was to lead my friends, neighbors, and others in my community to the Lord. I began teaching the Bible to small groups of people. Over time, those groups multiplied. Those who attended began to support me financially, which enabled me to go on radio. Little by little, my vision was expanding. Before long, I sensed God nudging me to go on television. Soon, we were reaching communities across America.

In 1976, God increased my desire again, this time directing me to reach souls worldwide. He gave me a verse of Scripture, Isaiah 11:9, which says: "For the earth shall be full of the knowledge of the LORD as the waters cover the sea" (NKJV). Today, Sarah and I are "covering the earth with the Word" together.

We regularly hold meetings in faraway places, some of them with strange-sounding names. Tens of thousands—yes, even hundreds of thousands—of people attend our meetings, and we are privileged to witness God's power in ways so magnificent I can hardly express them in words.

As I look back, I recognize that God increased *my capacity* and *my vision and heart for the lost* simultaneously. The more

I gave away what God put in me, the more I had to give. The more I gave, the more I saw the need to give.

This principle of God is true for every person. Start where you are with what you have to give. He will help you give generously with a cheerful heart and He will multiply what you give to bless the world now and for generations to come.

UNLIMITED ENLARGEMENT

We never reach our full capacity to give and receive because God always has more! His storehouse is unlimited. His ways and means of pouring out His blessing are unlimited. The same is true for a family. No family ever reaches its full capacity to impact the world, because God is continually increasing its capacity.

Be quick to thank God for the ways in which He has enlarged your capacity to give and receive. Keep your eyes open to the opportunities He presents to you, however miniscule they may seem to be. Remember, everything starts with a seed and the harvest is virtually unlimited.

A woman once told us: "I worked for fifty cents an hour when I was sixteen. I made ten dollars a week in my part-time job. I now receive five hundred dollars an hour for the consulting services I render to businesses. I only work about four eight-hour days a week on average, but that's sixteen thousand dollars a week. Even with a few weeks off a year to vacation with my family, I make a very good income—and it's all God. He sends my clients. He gives me the opportunities. I could never engineer or make happen all God has done."

She continued, "I was taught as a child to give tithes and offerings. I've been doing that since I was eight years old and received my first allowance. When I was sixteen, I was able to give a dollar a week into the offering plate, and I usually gave two dollars because I wanted to give an offering as well. Looking back, I never felt any great need in my life. The fourteen dollars a week I had left over was plenty to buy the things I needed and wanted as a sixteen-year-old. Now I'm able to give much more, and I get a great deal of joy in doing that. The truth is, I don't *need* sixteen thousand dollars a week to live a good life. Even after taxes, and even after paying all my bills and being generous with my family members, I am able to give about 40 percent of what I earn to various ministries that extend the gospel."

What a wonderful example of this principle of increased capacity! But there's even more. This woman then said, "You know, I once read about a man named LeTourneau—the founder of LeTourneau College—who ended up giving away 90 percent of what he made. He lived on 10 percent of his income. I've made it a goal in my life to be able to do what he did within the next ten years if the Lord hasn't returned by then."

Please understand this woman did not share this information with us proudly or in a bragging way. We had to practically pull this story out of her. She lives a humble, unassuming life, and very few people would ever guess she earns what she earns in a given month or year. She lives a life of high quality, but she does not flaunt her blessing.

Furthermore, as she shared how God has blessed her, she was radiant. Nothing about her giving was a burden to her; she did not feel any weight of obligation or pressure. She was delighted to give.

God enlarges your capacity to give and to receive *over time.* Be encouraged by that. What you cannot receive today you will one day be able to receive. What you cannot give today you will one day be able to give. God will produce that increase in you, both individually and in your family.

DIVINE INTERRUPTION

Consider which actions you can take to enlarge your capacity to receive. Can you step up your financial giving? Be more generous with your time? Be more helpful at work? Be a more loving spouse and more patient parent? Decide which items are your top three and purpose to do them over the next three months. Refresh your list periodically and stick to your goals—then get ready for your harvest!

10

Send the Devil Packing

Have you ever felt like saying to someone, "Get off my back! Get out of my life! Get your mitts off what is rightfully mine!"

You might regret saying these things to people, but they are excellent statements to make with your faith when the devil tries to assault your inheritance as a child of God. Make no mistake, the devil's mission is to eat away at what is rightfully yours, in every area of life. He will use every method at his disposal, unless you stop him. Peter explains:

"Be careful! Watch out for attacks from the Devil, your great enemy. He prowls around like a roaring lion, looking for some victim to devour. Take a firm stand against him, and be strong in your faith" (1 Pet. 5:8–9).

Devour is a strong word. To devour is to completely destroy, devastate, consume, or obliterate. You *devour* when you are ravenous. In that state, you don't just pick at a slice of pie, you *devour* it. That's the goal of the devil when it comes to your life. He has a voracious appetite for destruction. He comes to devour your family, your testimony, your destiny. The devil doesn't just want to pinch you, slap you around, or trip you up. He wants to *destroy* you. The Bible says he roars against us like a lion "looking for some victim to devour."

Insight from Sarah

First Peter 5:8 describes the devil's tactics as he stalks his potential victims. Peter says as the devil approaches his prey, he roars like a lion. Tigers do the same thing. A very interesting scientific study gives us more insight into the workings of the tiger's roar in the animal kingdom.

Like lions, tigers are fierce predators. They are quick and strong, and given the opportunity, they will tear their prey to pieces. But the tiger's attack begins before he sinks his teeth into his intended victim. His attack begins, not with physical contact, but with his ferocious roar. The sound distracts his victim, causing him to freeze rather than run.

As experts studied the tiger's hunting techniques further, they learned that the tiger's roar emits subsonic waves. These sound waves "paralyze" the prey, delaying the victim's flight just long enough for the tiger to gain the advantage.

This roar is essentially a deception. The tiger uses it to delay his victim's reactions, thereby compromising the prey's ability to escape the attack. In this way, the predator has accomplished his objective, just by making a sound.

The tiger's roar is intimidating, but it is not the animal's roar that consumes its prey. When the devil roars, tell him about the limits of his ability. Remind him that God's power is without match. Stand firm in God's power and you will overcome every demonic attack. The Bible tells us how: "Humble yourselves before God. Resist the Devil, and he will flee from you. Draw close to God, and God will draw close to you" (James 4:7–8).

When the devil raises his voice, God tells us to humble ourselves before Him, to put ourselves completely in His hands. From that place of protection and power, we can resist the devil and the devil will be forced to flee. We are not on the defense—but on the offense. God doesn't ask us to flee from the devil, He asks us to stand up to the devil.

Because God's Word instructs us to resist, we can be sure God has equipped us to wage war successfully. He has given us mighty spiritual weapons, but these weapons are not our own; they are God's. "We are human, but we don't wage war with human plans and methods. We use God's mighty weapons, not mere worldly weapons, to knock down the Devil's strongholds" (2 Cor. 10:3–4).

Hallmark of Blessing #3:
Victory Over the Destroyer

God has given us spiritual weapons and authority to overcome the devil's attempts to devour us. He has purchased and covered us with *the blood of Jesus*; He has given us the authority to speak in *the name of Jesus*; and He has given us *His Word* to speak into every situation we face. At the crux of this spiritual arsenal is the assurance that it is *God's will* for us to triumph over the attacks of the enemy and live a blessed life.

In reality, Jesus has *already* sent the devil packing! Jesus laid down His life for us and then rose from the dead. Therefore, we have available "God's mighty weapons . . . to knock down the Devil's strongholds." Jesus has made the ultimate provision for you and your family to enjoy a robust, abundant life, a life in which "death is swallowed up in victory" (1 Cor. 15:54 KJV).

KNOW YOUR ENEMY

There's an old saying that the first step to defeating an enemy is to know him and know what he is up to. Jesus gives us insight into the nature of our enemy, saying, "The thief's purpose is to steal and kill and destroy" (John 10:10).

Stealing, killing, and destroying are exactly what the enemy is up to. Let's take a closer look at these three specific behaviors of the devil against our spiritual rewards in Christ Jesus:

• *Steal.*
We suffer loss only when things we *value* are taken from us. The devil will come after anything you value deeply. He makes strong attempts to steal your time, your sanity, your God-given talents and spiritual gifts, your loved ones, and your thoughts.

• *Kill.*
Certainly the devil would like to kill us physically, either through illness or accident. But until the day we die, the devil also seeks to "kill" us in other ways. He wants to destroy your godly relationships. He wants to subvert godly friendships, marriages, and families. He wants to taint any relationship you may have with "spiritual children"—those you have led to Christ or those you are teaching or mentoring in the faith. Perhaps more than anything else, he wants to kill your God-given dreams.

• *Destroy.*

The devil will seek to destroy anything you have established or achieved. He especially moves against your reputation and your ability to influence others for Christ. He will give his strongest effort to destroying any fruit from your ministry.

To successfully resist the devil and his methods of destruction, we must use all the spiritual weapons at our disposal. First and foremost, we must rest in the finished work of the cross by faith, receiving all of the blessings Jesus' sacrifice has already provided for us.

Victory over Sickness and Disease.

Jesus' provision for us includes healing. There is no disease, known or as yet undiscovered, more powerful than God's healing touch. Over the years, we have heard about countless miraculous healings, one more dazzling than the next. Recently, we heard from Kristie Lamb. Her testimony is so outstanding it could change your life.

Kristie's problems began after the birth of her second child. She began to lose vision in her left eye and to have persistent headaches. She went to see an ophthalmologist, who referred her to a neurologist, who immediately ordered an MRI. Kristie worked in a hospital so she knew immediately when the neurologist's report couldn't be given to her over the phone, it was something serious. As she faced her appointment with the physician, she was scared. She feared a brain tumor, so when the doctor told her she had multiple sclerosis, she actually felt a little relieved.

Kristie was very vulnerable in her letter to us. She told us at that point, rather than rely on God, she began to rely on herself. She withdrew from other people, including her husband. She even stopped praying. She went into deeper and deeper depression until while she was out driving one day, she snapped. With her two young children in the van with her, she began to drive faster and faster until she was going more than a hundred miles an hour. She fully intended to create a horrible traffic accident that she was sure she wouldn't survive . . . and neither would her children.

Then, for no explainable reason, her van suddenly began to slow down without her ever hitting the brakes. She pulled the vehicle to the side of the road, where she cried uncontrollably for some time. Finally she made it home safely.

In the days following, Kristie continued to work and function to some degree of normalcy, but one night at about two o'clock, she began to cry and couldn't seem to stop. Her husband awoke and she told him about the incident with her van and asked his forgiveness for what she had thought about doing.

Her husband did a wonderful thing. He held her and forgave her and then began to pray for her. He took authority in the name of Jesus over her suicidal thoughts and the depression, and together, they began to search the Word for Scriptures on healing. Kristie began to write out specific Scriptures she found as she searched the Bible, beginning with Isaiah 53:4–5: "It was our weaknesses he carried; it was our sorrows that weighed him down. And we thought his troubles were a punishment from God for his own sins! But he was wounded and crushed for our sins. He was beaten that we might have peace. He was whipped, and we were healed!"

Kristie taped this passage of Scripture and other verses all over the house so she saw the Word of God wherever she looked, including the bedroom, bathroom mirror, refrigerator door, sun visor in her car, and also in her locker at work. She filled her mind with the Word of God and began to reach out to other people, including her father, from whom she had been estranged.

In the weeks that followed, Kristie's vision returned but she still had weakness. She didn't give in to the weakness—instead, she continued to follow God's leading and saturate her mind and heart with the Word of God. Then one day she realized she had been symptom-free for three months. About that same time, her neurologist asked her to come in to discuss a new medication for multiple sclerosis.

Kristie and her husband prayed about her taking that medication, and she decided that if this medication was God's pathway for her healing, she was willing to take it. First, however, she decided to get a second opinion. The second neurologist, as could be expected, wanted to conduct another MRI of her brain and also conduct a complete neurological exam before he made his recommendation. Prior to those more extensive tests, this physician did an eye exam and asked Kristie if she was sure it was her left eye that had gone blind. Kristie's husband roared with laughter as the doctor looked from eye to eye and couldn't tell a difference. Kristie had the other tests the neurologist recommended, but the MRI and other reports showed no evidence of multiple sclerosis in her body!

That was twelve years ago. Kristie has never had any further symptoms of MS.

Is God your healer?

Absolutely!

More than your healer, is He your health?

Yes! And all-powerfully so, because the Cross and the Resurrection have already happened—the price was already paid!

Protection from Natural Catastrophes

Whatever crisis rears its head in your life, resist the discouragement and despair the enemy will try to bring. Stand firm in God's promised provision. Trust Him to protect and provide for you in storms, floods, fires, and other natural catastrophes. If you suffer loss or damage, rely on God to help you rebuild your life in a way that is in keeping with His natural and spiritual laws.

Not long ago we heard about a young couple who lived on the coastline of California. They did something very few people do: they asked the Lord specifically, "Are we living where you want us to live?" The answer was a clear "No!"

They then asked the Lord to show them where He wanted them to live, and He led them to what they now call their dream house on the East Coast, more than three thousand miles from their California home overlooking the Pacific.

Three months after they moved, the area they left in California was ravaged by torrential rains and mudslides. This couple has no doubt that when they humbled themselves and asked for direction, God gave them a clear word *in advance* so they might avoid a disaster.

Preservation of Joy and Peace

The devil knows if he can cause you to live on a "knife's edge" emotionally, he can distract you from your destiny. One of the ways he does this is by exploiting your senses: what your eyes see, what your ears hear, what you touch, taste, and smell. He will entice you with fantasies that play on your desires and emotional needs, and he will tempt you to exercise your God-given free will for your own destruction.

Emotionally, there are three patterns of behaviors that, left unchecked, will dissolve our joy and peace. The Bible describes these as being part of the curse detailed in Deuteronomy 28. Bear in mind that those who claim Jesus Christ as their Savior need not be victimized by these behaviors, because they have been delivered from the curse. (See Galatians 3:13.)

Deuteronomy 28:20 says this: "The LORD will send on you

cursing, confusion, and rebuke in all that you set your hand to do, until you are destroyed and until you perish quickly, because of the wickedness of your doings in which you have forsaken Me" (NKJV).

• *Cursings.*

This word in Deuteronomy 28:20 does not refer to a generational curse. Nor does it refer to swearing or using curse words. Cursings, in this case, are unprovoked and unwarranted threats. The person who hears threatening words often feels as if he or she has virtually no power to change the situation.

• *Vexations or Confusion.*

A vexation is a taunt. *Vexations* is a word which refers to *continual* taunting. Hannah was a woman who endured vexations from a woman the Bible calls her rival, Peninnah, who "made fun of Hannah because the LORD had closed her womb" (1 Sam. 1:6). Vexations produce extreme anxiety. They cause a person to live on the edge of frustration and the brink of tears.

• *Rebukes or Disillusionment.*

Rebukes are severe put-downs. (See also Deuteronomy 28:15.) Sometimes a rebuke is warranted—there are times when you need to tell someone to "back off" and stop trespassing across certain physical or emotional boundaries. But in other cases, rebukes are uttered by a bully who wants to exert power over or manipulate other people. Bullies criticize others in hopes of making themselves look better and keeping others from succeeding.

Rebukes of this kind often come in the form of rejection. The person who suffers an ongoing barrage of criticism and rejection usually feels anger. If that anger is vented, it can become explosive rage. If the anger is stuffed inside and unresolved, it can become seething bitterness and hatred. Think of the terrible consequences, emotionally, physically, and relationally that can result from these simmering emotions over a lifetime.

Nothing good comes from ongoing cursings, vexations, and rebukes. These behaviors not only destroy personal peace and joy, but they can obliterate the peace and joy in a family, perpetuating patterns of unhealthy interaction. People who live in this type of emotional environment eventually shrivel inside. How awful it can be when feelings of self-worth and self-respect dissipate, opening the door to self-destructive tendencies that can spiral out of a person's control.

Hear this, because it can transform your life: we are not doomed to live chaotic, fear-filled lives. We are not victims, but victors, people of great value bought with the precious blood of the Lamb of God, handpicked by Him, the apple of His eye. As Joel Osteen says in his sermon "The Power of Your Bloodline": "We are God's thoroughbreds and we have royal blood flowing through our veins!"

Jesus said:

Come to me, all of you who are weary and carry heavy burdens, and I will give you rest. (Matthew 11:28)

For God so loved the world that he gave his only Son, so that everyone who believes in him will not perish but have eternal life. God did not send his Son into the world to condemn it, but to save it (John 3:16–17)

I am leaving you with a gift — peace of mind and heart. And the peace I give isn't like the peace the world gives. So don't be troubled or afraid. (John 14:27)

We must speak these words over our lives because the truth of God always nullifies the threats, taunts, and traumatic words of the devil. We must speak truth to our loved ones, never bullying, making fun, or putting them down. God holds us accountable for our words; therefore, it is important to set the tone for our families' everyday interaction.

Decide and affirm often:

- In our home, we choose a gentle tone of voice and godly words to bring encouragement to others and promote a sense of safety and security.
- Our children speak lovingly, never taunting one another.
- We praise and encourage our children, balancing constructive criticism with affirmation.
- Our discipline is based in love and understanding; we do not attempt to change our children's behavior by issuing threats.

Remember, it's never too late to initiate a pattern of blessing. It begins with a decision and it happens in a moment of time. And we are empowered by God's grace to do it.

The Outmanned, Underpowered Devourer

The devil is a defeated foe, because Jesus defeated him. The devil's fate has been sealed. But between today and the day of his final demise, he will continue his often subtle attempts to undermine your life.

The devil is the "accuser of our brethren" (Rev. 12:10 KJV). He accuses you by saying, "Just wait until the world finds out what you once did. Your reputation will take a fast slide downhill. You have no real integrity. Everything you think you've established is just a sham."

He stirs fear in your heart by saying, "You are losing your husband because you are such a lousy wife." "You are going to lose your wife because you are such a bad husband." "You are a failure when it comes to being a friend." "You're an incompetent parent." "You are a terrible witness for Christ." "Your ministry will never flourish. It will die."

Refuse these thoughts! Take them captive and respond to the accuser, "You are a liar and the father of all lies." Don't let the devil demean you or your reputation. And don't allow him to derail your ministry. Respond to his attacks with determination and good works.

When the devil accuses you, remind him who you are in Christ Jesus. Tell him Jesus is your Savior and therefore, your sins are forgiven, your past has been forgotten by God, and your future is securely in His hands. Tell him Jesus gives you all the worth you need, He says you are valuable beyond measure, and He loves you with an incalculable love. Tell him Jesus' opinion of you is all that matters.

Teach your child to do the same.

The Impact on Generational Blessings

How does this impact your family's generational blessings? You and your child are going to encounter people who are quick to tell you all your faults, point out all your failures, and to predict that anything good you attempt will fail.

When they do, say simply and with a calm voice, "That is not the truth." You don't need to debate the issue; simply redirect your thoughts to the goodness of God. Refuse to allow a lie to take root in you. Remain focused on God and how much He loves you. Train your children to follow suit; show them how to hold God's Word as the standard by which they measure the words and actions of others.

Insight from Sarah

A few years ago I took mountain-biking lessons. It was great fun, but it was very challenging, too. The terrain was unpredictable, full of brush and small outcroppings that could trip you up at every turn. The inclines that make mountain biking exciting also add to the danger. It's a game of inches; to stay on the bike and out of harm's way you've got to be extremely focused. A small mistake can get you hurt.

My instructor had lots of experience and was able to accurately assess my performance, for better or worse. He didn't candy-coat his input. It was his job to train me to be a safe mountain biker and he took his job seriously.

He taught me lots of good techniques and gave me loads of useful tips. One lesson he taught me really sticks out in my mind. I was having trouble negotiating curves. Even though I was concentrating hard on all the variables—assessing the angles, the pitch, and my speed—I consistently lost control of the bike.

That's when my instructor explained the concept of looking ahead of the curve. Here's how it works: when you're about to enter any kind of turn, you have to resist the desire to focus on the curve itself. You already know it's there. Instead, you must focus on what is coming up *after* the curve. If you do, you'll stay on the bike, because where you're looking is where you will go.

You've probably had a similar experience while driving. If you turn your head to look at something alongside the road, the car follows you in that direction.

Our thought life operates the same way. When we focus on the accusations of the devil or the less-than-positive things people say about us, we begin to move in the direction of the lies we entertain. The way to move past deception is to *look* past it. Concentrate on the bigger picture: the truth of God's Word and all it says about who you *really* are.

Where you're looking is where you will go.

Declare the blessings of God over yourself and your family, by speaking aloud His very words:

> *We belong to Christ, and we are blessed with every spiritual blessing in the heavenly realms. Our hearts are flooded with the light of God and we understand the wonderful future He has for us. No weapon that is formed against us will prosper and we condemn every tongue that rises in judgment against us. Jesus carried our weaknesses and our sorrows, and because He was beaten, we have peace.*
>
> *(See 1 Corinthians 3:23; Ephesians 1:3, 18; Isaiah 54:17, 53:4–5.)*

Develop your own list of scriptural blessings to speak over your family. Make it a point to verbally bless your children often and encourage them to speak God's promises over you. As they hear words of blessing over and over again, they will become familiar with the truth of God's love. It will strengthen them from within and provide the sturdy foundation they need to send the devil packing.

POWER POINT

If you make it a practice to measure life's events, the words of others, thought patterns, and everyday challenges against the standard of God's Word, you will undermine the devil's strategies to steal, kill, and destroy, and you will establish a model of Christian living—a legacy for the generations after you.

11

Live Fully in the "Land" God Has Given You

The story is told of a ten-year-old girl who went to visit her grandparents one summer. The grandparents lived on a small farm and this girl loved to work in the large vegetable garden they planted. She helped them hoe the garden and pick the vegetables all summer. Then, on the last week of her visit, she asked her grandparents if she could clear a piece of ground next to the barn to plant a *flower* garden.

"It's too late to plant flowers right now," her grandfather explained.

"But can I clear the ground so I can plant flowers the first day I come back next year?" the girl asked.

The grandparents agreed.

The little girl cleared away a piece of ground and built a little picket fence around it. She could hardly wait to return the next summer.

Her first day back on the farm the next year she went out behind the barn and quickly returned to the house in disgust.

"It's a mess!" she said. "All of that ground I cleared is filled with weeds, weeds, weeds!"

Her grandfather said to her, "Honey, your grandma and I talked about your garden and we knew that we could keep clearing the ground all fall, winter, and spring, but we wanted you to learn an important lesson. It isn't enough just to clear away the weeds. You have to plant something good immediately where the weeds were growing, or the weeds will come back. This summer you are starting on your garden the first day you are here. The minute you finish clearing the weeds, we'll plant flowers. In a few weeks, you'll have wonderful flowers. Don't ever forget, when you pull a weed, you have to plant a seed."

How true that is in all areas of our lives. When you pull a weed, plant a seed!

Weeding and planting, whether in the natural or spiritual realms, are just the beginning. To protect our harvest, we must maintain the ground—that is, we must rule and reign over everything God has entrusted to us, including the physical space He has given us to occupy, the things He has called us to do, and time He has given us to live.

Hallmark of Blessing #4:
A Pleasant or Delightful Land

God desires that your "land" would be a delight, a representation of your inheritance in Him, the pleasant territory described by David.

> LORD, you alone are my inheritance,
> my cup of blessing.
> You guard all that is mine.

The land you have given me is a pleasant land.
What a wonderful inheritance!
(PSALM 16:5–6)

Your "land" includes the time and space allotted to you by God. When we are faithful to God's commands and manage our territory well, it becomes a beacon to others, a testimony of God's goodness and favor. Moses said the nations would stand in awe of God's people because of their unique relationship with the Almighty.

> *If you obey the commands of the LORD your God and walk in his ways, the LORD will establish you as his holy people as he solemnly promised to do. Then all the nations of the world will see that you are a people claimed by the LORD, and they will stand in awe of you. (Deuteronomy 28:9–10)*

God has given each of us a territory to occupy. The upkeep of our "delightful land" falls to us; it is not accidental, but a matter of assuming our rightful authority. In God's eyes, what goes on in your territory is your responsibility.

NATURAL ORDER THROUGH SUPERNATURAL POWER

Our authority as believers can be exerted only through the Holy Spirit, by faith. Genuine, effective faith supersedes the limits of the intellect and overpowers the boundaries of the physical. Pastor Yonggi Cho, pastor of more than 750,000 (the largest congregation in the world), has lived by this kind of faith for decades. He calls it "fourth-dimension living."

If the phrase *fourth dimension* sounds ethereal to you, be assured that the concept of fourth-dimension living is neither complicated nor mystical. Very simply, the natural world consists of *time*, *space*, and *material*—what Dr. Cho calls the *third dimension*. The planets, the seven continents, our homes, our physical bodies exist in time, take up space, and consist of matter.

Much of the territory God has commanded us to occupy is found within this third dimension. God has given us *natural* means by which to govern our physical territory. When the roof leaks, we fix it with manual labor and the right materials. These are third-dimension solutions designed to address a common, third-dimension problem. Fixing the roof is, at first glance, a mundane activity. Yet, from a kingdom perspective, it is an important action because we honor God by stewarding, or *taking good care of*, all He gives us by any suitable means.

Still, we cannot overcome the challenges we face in the physical world exclusively through finite, natural means. To live overcoming lives, we must operate *above* the natural plane in the realm of the spiritual.

The Bible account of the Creation illustrates the exertion of God's supernatural authority over the physical world. Using Pastor Cho's vocabulary, fourth-dimension faith was applied to bring order to the third-dimension world: "The earth was empty, a formless mass cloaked in darkness. And the Spirit of God was hovering over its surface. Then God said, 'Let there be light,' and there was light" (Gen. 1:2–3).

The earth is described in this passage as being in a state of chaos; it lacked form and was shrouded in darkness. Then God commanded progressive stages of order to be established, because order was part of God's vision for His creation.

He began by saying, "Let there be light." Because God exists in and speaks from the fourth dimension, light came the instant God commanded it. Over the course of six days, God's words and the power of the Holy Spirit brought a disorganized world into perfect harmony.

How do we bring our "world" into alignment? Very much the same way God did. We have the Holy Spirit within us and God's Word available to us. As we speak His words in faith and accept our responsibility to take authority in our "land," we begin to frame our world and rise above the level of the third dimension. In this way, we are responding to our circumstances in fourth-dimension ways.

1. God's Word.

God's Word expresses God's thoughts. If we answer third-dimension challenges with third-dimension thinking, the circumstances will overtake us instead of the other way around. How do we get our thoughts and words in line with God's? By "being renewed in the spirit of our minds." (See Ephesians 4:23.) Explain to your children what it means to renew one's mind and show them how to do it. Find interesting, age-appropriate ways for them to read the Scriptures and learn about God's ways.

2. Supernatural Vision.

We speak the Word confidently when we have a clear picture of what God's will is. "Where there is no vision [no redemptive revelation of God], the people perish" (Prov. 29:18 AMP). When your world is coming unglued, a vision from God will provide stability. It will undergird you with a blueprint of your future. Encourage your children to seek God's plan for their lives by seeking *Him*. Provide constructive outlets for their unique gifts and talents. This will foster self-discovery and a desire to realize their God-given dreams.

3. Fourth-Dimension Faith.

"Faith is the substance of things hoped for, the evidence of things not seen" (Heb. 11:1 NKJV). Faith is not activated by what is evident in the natural realm. Instead, faith rests in what God says *will be*, so when we release our faith in earnest, we expect circumstances to change. Help your children to apply their faith to real-life situations important to them. Then teach them to recognize God's answers. Help them rehearse their testimonies; it will build their faith and trust in God.

4. Prayer.

For prayer to be fully effective, we pray according to God's Word and by the leading of the Holy Spirit. Even when we are at a complete loss for what to pray, we can rely upon divine guidance: "The Holy Spirit helps us in our distress. For we don't even know what we should pray for, nor how we should pray. But the Holy Spirit prays for us with groanings that cannot be expressed in words" (Rom. 8:26).

Engage your children in times of prayer. You might help them to develop personalized, scriptural prayers to address their particular needs and circumstances. Encourage them to seek the Holy Spirit's guidance in how to pray effectively in every situation.

5. Language.

To live in the realm of the supernatural, it is important to choose your words with care. Be careful not to sabotage your petitions to God with everyday speech that contradicts what you have prayed. Help your children to avoid undermining their prayers; remind them to guard against idle or destructive words and thoughtless conversation.

Hallmark of Blessing #5
Words That Speak to a Blessed Future

God gave us His Word not only to guide, but to bless. He also gave us the power inherent in speech. One of the profound joys of generation blessing is to speak the Word of God over our children and grandchildren and know that it will be fruitful in the days, years, and generations to come. "So shall My word be that goes forth from My mouth; it shall not return to Me void, but it shall accomplish what I please, and it shall prosper in the thing for which I sent it" (Isaiah 55:11 NKJV).

FAITH FOR YOUR GENERATIONS

Every promise of God is received by faith. When God told Abram he would become the father of a great nation, Abram had no physical evidence to support what God said. Quite the opposite: all physical signs seemed to contradict God's words. Yet we know that Abram continued to trust God, even after decades passed and nothing changed. *That is faith* and the Bible says it is impossible to please God without it. (Heb. 11:6) "[Abram] did not waver at the promise of God through unbelief, but was strengthened in faith, giving glory to God, and being fully convinced that what He had promised He was also able to perform. And therefore 'it was accounted to him for righteousness.'" (Rom. 4:20–22 NKJV).

In believing, Abram glorified God. His enduring faith was a signal that, above all else, Abram wanted what God wanted. As a result, Abram lived to see God's blessing manifested in his life and thousands of years later, *we* partake in the generation blessing that began with Abram.

Until Jesus returns, your generations can reap the harvest of this ancient blessing because your faith in Jesus grafts you into Abraham's lineage:

> *"You Gentiles, who were branches from a wild olive tree, were grafted in. So now you also receive the blessing God has promised Abraham and his children, sharing in God's rich nourishment of his special olive tree"* (Rom. 11:17).

While the promise was given long ago, it is your trust in God today that will empower you to make good choices and *receive* the promised blessings. Your faith will enable you to be proactive, to do the things that make an eternal difference, to make good decisions even when it costs you something, to love when you're hurting, to discipline consistently in order to enjoy God's reward: a godly heritage for your family and your community.

These are godly ways in which you take ownership of your life and family. This is where the mettle of your faith is tested, the place where theory becomes reality, where authority is not just talked about but implemented.

There are some simple things you can do to maintain your authority over your territory and rip out the weeds that will try to grow in your land. Much of the maintenance has to do with promoting the right atmosphere by carefully choosing what you will tolerate in your home or workplace.

• **Make wholesome speech the standard in your home— and expect your children to uphold the standard.** Object to dirty, racially demeaning, or otherwise inappropriate jokes at home or in the workplace. If someone asks why you take exception, gently explain your position, not with religious catchwords but in simple language. Chances are they will respect your honesty.

• **Filter the sources that influence the heart.** Thwart the entrance of ungodly lyrics or media tirades that assault your peace. Avoid concerts by artists who release violent or sexually explicit lyrics and protect your children or teenagers from such events.

• **Intercept messages that mold the mind.** Monitor television programs and other media accessible from your home. Be alert to messages of immorality or violence that violate your territory via the Internet or other electronic media.

It is up to you to guard the threshold of your home. Your children may not always appreciate your vigilance, but you are not called to make popular decisions—you are called to take a stand on behalf of your family. Little Johnny's room may be his room *to an extent*, but his room is in *your house* and you are the authority figure God appointed to protect your territory.

Set rules. Set limits. And stick to them.

❧

Insight from Sarah

My husband, Reece, and I are careful about who speaks into our lives and into the lives of our children.

Especially when it comes to our kids, we make sure we're both in agreement with any person who is teaching them, regardless of the subject. We want them to grow in the areas of their gifts and talents, but not at the expense of their souls.

We carefully monitor the messages aired in our household, whether through the TV, books, games, or our own speech. It didn't take us long to figure out we couldn't control *everything*. So, when we encounter something that doesn't support our family values, we talk about it with our kids. We take a few minutes to explain why something they saw or heard doesn't fit what we believe. In the long run, this will help them make better choices. It also satisfies their curiosity about why we are setting limits.

God gave us three children in quick succession, so our household is an active one. You can imagine the level of our kids' combined energy. They love to play and laugh. They are adventurous and, like all kids, they are curious. We do our best to give them the latitude, within reason, to speak their minds, to explore their world, and to have fun.

At the same time, we work to make our home a place of security and peace. Our children know who the parents are and understand that Reece and I are obliged to obey God, even when it means disappointing them.

Raising children isn't easy, but it is rewarding—sleepless nights and all!

Insight from Marilyn

I agree with Sarah and I encourage you to be a close guardian when it comes to who teaches, coaches, befriends, or otherwise influences your children.

When Sarah was in school, I was tipped off by another parent that a particular teacher seemed to be paying a little too much attention to Sarah. Normally I would have thought this teacher just loved my daughter and thought she was as wonderful as I thought she was. The more I watched the situation, however, the more concerned I became. This teacher was displaying behaviors that weren't normal for a teacher—in today's language, this teacher was on the verge of becoming predatory. I prayed about the situation, but I also took action. I called the principal of the school and insisted that he address the situation.

The teacher backed off and Sarah continued to excel in both her studies and in her athletic pursuits.

Don't assume that because you send your children to a good school or get involved in the right club that your children are automatically safe. Sexual abuse is rampant in modern society. All too frequently people in authority—teachers, clergy, and caretakers—take advantage of children. Be aware of who has access to your children and be alert to any inappropriate activity.

The devil, of course, has no interest in destroying the weeds in your garden or in halting the negative things occurring in your life or home. He seeks, rather, to destroy the good fruit that comes from your ground. Therefore, you must guard your land against encroachment.

Protect your child from impure associations. Choose whom, even at the earliest ages, your children will play with, whether at your home, a neighbor's home, or at school. Know where your children go. Scout out what goes on in their friends' homes before you agree to let them spend time there. Rely on the Holy Spirit to point out issues of concern. Help your children understand your choices as to which friends make the grade in your eyes; it will help them to do the same as they get older.

Choose carefully whom you invite to be a guest in your home, and especially whom you allow to stay overnight or to be with your child when you aren't present. Choose caregivers, such as babysitters, nannies, and after-school supervisors, with care. These authority figures carry a great deal of influence over your child.

You are the king or queen of your home. As you take full reign over your territory, trust God to bring forth hearty fruit in the good environment you have created. When you take authority over the physical space you have been given, you are setting a strong example for your children and grandchildren. Children like what is pure and real and they want to be protected. They like what is beautiful and peaceful. They will choose the shelter of what feels secure and safe. Accept wholeheartedly the leadership responsibilities God has given you, and you will create a home environment that breeds generational blessing.

TAKE AUTHORITY OVER THE TIME GOD HAS GIVEN YOU

Every person gets twenty-four hours in a day, yet too often we find ourselves saying, "I don't have time." The truth is, if you consistently feel as though time is scarce when it comes to doing the important things, you may have overloaded your schedule or procrastinated in some way.

Malachi talks about the "grapes [that] shrivel before they are ripe" (Mal. 3:11). This is fruit that is out of God's timing. Farmers tell us unripe fruit drops from a tree or vine before its time primarily because of stressors. The stressor might be weather conditions, an assault by insects, or bad farming practices. What a metaphor for today's society. Many are "dropping" before their time, in exhaustion or death, because of extreme stress.

Doctors will tell you stress is the most insidious cause of disease in our world today. How we handle our schedules — whether we attempt to do too much in too little time, or fail to take time to reflect, rest, and relax—is directly related to the level of stress we experience. Stress can show up in a number of ways:

- Stress makes a person more prone to anger.
- Stress creates frustration that robs a person of joy.
- Stress can fracture a relationship.
- Stress can undermine faith.

Prayerfully consider the level of stress in your life and then pull out your daily calendar. Start saying no to things that are not as important in God's eyes as you once thought. Has God prompted you to be involved to the extent you are involved? Ask yourself: *Has God led me to take on all the responsibilities and obligations that drive my schedule?*

Well-meaning people often take on obligations for the wrong reasons. They may have failed to set healthy boundaries in their relationships with others or may feel unduly responsible for others. An overactive lifestyle should send up a red flag: busyness can be used to mask a feeling of emptiness or to satisfy an emotional need better met through intimacy with God.

Each moment of time is a seed to sow. If we are constantly in a rush or continually feel stressed out, we rarely produce our best work or do our best parenting. Whether we have noticed or not, our stressed-out frame of mind negatively affects our families. We risk dropping our "good fruit" before its time.

When we're running on empty, we can miss out on the depth of relationship that results from sharing quality time with others. As the saying goes, children spell love T-I-M-E. They thrive on regular doses of quality time with Mom or Dad. Our spouses draw closer to us when we set aside daily time to listen and to share experiences with them. It takes time to be a good friend or to help someone in a time of need. Most precious of all, it takes time to enjoy a strong, intimate relationship with God.

Making time for others can be fun for you, too! It needn't be complicated. The whole family can get involved baking a favorite cake or putting a puzzle together. Schedule a family ice cream break after weekend chores. Have fun experimenting with different ingredients to create unique sundaes. Your children will be motivated to participate and everyone will enjoy the conversation.

BALANCE WORK AND PLAY

When evaluating your overall schedule, cutting the overload is a good start, but have you thought about reintroducing activities that bring you enjoyment? Maybe you love gardening but have been too stressed out to enjoy it. Setting aside an hour or two each week would not only bring you enjoyment and relieve stress; it could turn your garden into a special space the whole family can enjoy.

Ask the Lord to show you the balance He desires for you to have between work and recreation, between exertion and rest, between input and output. Then, trust God to give you peace as you live out each day according to *His* schedule.

You are called to live a blessed life, an energetic, productive, exuberant life savored and lived to the full, a life of diverse interests and opportunities, a life to be embraced and enjoyed, a life worth living. Solomon talks about this life: "My son, forget not my law or teaching, but let your heart keep my commandments; for length of days and years of a life [worth living] and tranquility [inward and outward and continuing through old age till death], these shall they add to you" (Prov. 3:1–2 AMP).

God's desire as we obey His commandments is that all the ground under our control will produce good fruit, and that the fruit of our lives will fully ripen and be of maximum value. Believe for God's best as you take authority over your territory and your time.

VALUE A GODLY REPUTATION

In order to exercise our God-given authority, we must develop a godly reputation based upon good character and a track record of producing good work. People love to be around other people who are trustworthy, loving, and known for doing their best. We are drawn to people who do good things for the right reasons.

There's a reciprocal quality evident in those who cultivate a good reputation, they gravitate to other reputable people and they do things that build up the reputation of others.

Value Reputable Associations

The book of Proverbs commands us to:

- Align ourselves with those who are wise and avoid the pitfalls of associating with those who are foolish.
- Link ourselves with those who are diligent and hardworking instead of those who are dishonest or lazy.
- Cultivate relationships with those who are moral and steer clear of those who are unprincipled.

The apostle Paul gave very clear instruction to the early church: "Have no fellowship with the unfruitful works of darkness, but rather reprove them" (Eph. 5:11 KJV). Paul did not say we shouldn't *witness* to those who are in darkness. He said that we are not to have *fellowship* with them.

Honor What Is Reputable

A second major way to establish a good reputation is to applaud what is honorable in others. Give some thought to this. There are likely dozens of examples in your own life supporting these aspects of sowing and reaping:

- What you say about other people is going to be what is said about you.
- What you do for others is what others are going to do for you.
- What you applaud in others will be what others applaud in you.
- What you reward will be what you will be rewarded for.

Insight from Marilyn

When my husband, Wally, and I were assistant pastors of a church in Texas, we encountered a church secretary who gossiped a great deal and was bitter about many things. She generally had a bad attitude. Wally and I were young and this was our first experience in the ministry. We listened to this woman, and before we knew what was happening, we had allowed her negative words about the pastor to fill our own spirits, minds, and emotions. We began to speak negatively about him, too—not publicly, but certainly in the privacy of our own home. This man hadn't hurt us in the least; in fact, he was good to us. Our words against him were totally unjustified, and even if they had been justified, they were wrong.

Later, when God called us to lead a church, we noticed people were doing to us what we did to that pastor. Do you know what I did? I repented! I said, "I will never disrespect the hand that feeds me. I will never do that again!" It is never right to pull down the reputation of another person. In the end, the only reputation you pull down is your own. Most devastating of all, your children will follow your example, and by tearing down the good name of others, they will debase their own.

Jesus gave very clear teaching about reciprocity:

- Do for others as you would like them to do for you. (Luke 6:31)
- Love your enemies! Do good to them! Lend to them! And don't be concerned that they might not repay. Then your reward from heaven will be very great, and you will truly be acting as children of the Most High, for he is kind to the unthankful and to those who are wicked. You must be compassionate, just as your Father is compassionate. (Luke 6:35–36)
- Stop judging others, and you will not be judged. Stop criticizing others, or it will all come back on you. If you forgive others, you will be forgiven. (Luke 6:37)

Honoring others honors the God who created them. Be quick to speak to your children about what is honorable. Talk to them about people who have lived exemplary lives. Build up your pastor and others in the eyes of your child.

Of course, no person should be held up as being a god. Human beings fail. Leaders, even spiritual leaders, sometimes disappoint us. But we also know human beings can achieve great things. Applaud good role models. Take the time to explain the accomplishments of honorable men and women. Get your children *excited* about doing good deeds and setting good examples.

Claim a Reputation as "Blessed!"

When you face challenges, *and we all do,* choose to focus on the positive side of the ledger. Help your children do the same. Adopt the mind-set that God has innumerable blessings for you and that, each day, you are increasingly blessed.

Talk about God's blessings with your children.

As a family, describe the blessings you have experienced.

Be on the lookout for God's blessings every day!

DIVINE INTERRUPTION

Are there any weeds growing in the land God has given you? If so, decide which seeds you should plant in their place. Remember, God has equipped you to be the authority in your home. Ask Him to help you assess your performance and establish new patterns of godliness and generation blessing that will reach beyond your years on the earth.

12

Experience All-Out Joy

The world desperately seeks happiness. We hear phrases such as these all the time:

- "I just want to be happy."
- "I don't care what my children do, as long as they are happy."
- "Do whatever will make you happy."

Many things in today's world are no longer evaluated as to whether they are right or wrong; instead society's primary guideline has become: will it make me happy or unhappy?

The obsession with happiness is partly attributable to the nature of happiness; it is external, circumstantial, and dependent upon factors often beyond a person's control. In a word, happiness is *fleeting*. The elation we feel today can dissipate tomorrow and when the emotional crash comes, too many unhappy souls respond by searching for the next fix.

Nonstop happiness is an unattainable goal. The endless pursuit of bliss is exhausting and even debilitating. What people really want is *joy*, a far more reliable and sustainable state. Joy springs from within. It is consistent. It doesn't depend upon situations or circumstances. Joy is spiritual by its very nature. Joy is one of the greatest hallmarks of a blessed life.

Hallmark of Blessing #6:
Bubbling-Over Joy

The prophet Isaiah described the proverbial "skip in the step" of a joyful person when he wrote, "You will go out in joy and be led forth in peace" (Isa. 55:12 NIV). In other words, the blessed person approaches the world with exuberance. He or she views life's challenges and opportunities with intense optimism and a positive attitude that cannot be explained to the unbeliever.

The spirit of the Christian is *alive*. It is accustomed to being joyful. It is effervescent with joy. Genuine joy breaks through the hard places or difficult times in our lives, just as an artesian spring forces its way through sturdy layers of rock and gushes onto the surface of the earth.

"This just isn't possible," you might be saying. "It's artificial."

Not so! Joy is the most genuine emotion a person can have, because it comes from Christ. It is a *gift* to your heart from His heart. Jesus spoke of the joy He gave to His followers, saying, "I have told them many things while I was with them so they would be filled with my joy" (John 17:13).

Jesus fills us with His joy when we read the Word and spend time with Him. You can't manufacture joy on your own; you *receive* it. Joy elevates your outlook and penetrates every decision, every choice, every creative idea, and every opinion you have.

Joy comes from the absolute assurance we are God's children, loved, accepted, and forgiven by Him. Paul explains it is God who gives us this assurance: "For his Holy Spirit speaks to us deep in our hearts and *tells us that we are God's children*" (Rom. 8:16, emphasis added).

Is something stealing *your* joy? Have you fully accepted the truth that God loves you, and God has forgiven you—completely?

Insight from Marilyn

There's no joy for me in admitting that many people on my father's side of the family had sour, overly serious, all-work-and-no-play attitudes. Life seemed to be all about discipline and constraint. This perspective affected my life to the point my mother once confronted me about being *driven*. I took issue with her at the time, but she was right.

More recently, God has transformed my all-work-and-no-play attitude into a love-to-work-*and*-enjoy-life approach, which is much better! During the time God dealt with me in this way, the Holy Spirit uncovered a root of despair deriving from a long-ago abusive relationship. Abuse is crushing. People who are into control or manipulation are often abusive, and abuse and joy just don't go together.

As I confronted the generational curses in my life, I had to recognize I did not have the joy God desired me to have. I had to confront the sexual abuse I experienced as a girl by a member of my extended family. Horrible memories were buried for decades. It was only when I unsealed them and invited God into that dark place in my heart that He was able to heal me, and I discovered a wonderful thing: when God heals, He frees!

In freeing me from the painful memories of abuse in my early years, God released me to feel joy as I had never felt it before. He showed me He had power over all that had overpowered me. With freedom and joy came a renewed ability to express my emotions with greater freedom.

If you don't have joy in your life today, ask God to show you why. If there's an area of abuse or pain deep in your past, open up those memories to your heavenly Father and ask Him to heal you and set you free.

ACCEPT GOD'S FORGIVENESS—COMPLETELY!

If you aren't experiencing abiding joy, is it possible you've never really asked God to forgive you? If that is the case, it's not too late! Admit to Him you feel guilty; confess to Him you have sinned (everyone has). Express to the God who knows and loves you that you desire to be forgiven. Confess your belief that Jesus suffered and died so your sins might be erased. And then receive the forgiveness that comes simply by believing.

Be Forgiven by God

Every spiritual benefit, including forgiveness, must be received by faith. Faith is rarely blind; faith is supported by what we know about God's character: He is trustworthy, loving, and wise. Our faith is also undergirded by God's assurance that He will do what He promised. For example, we know for a certainty that when we pray according to God's will, He hears and answers our prayer. "This is the confidence we have in approaching God: that if we ask anything according to his will, he hears us. And if we know that he hears us—whatever we ask—we know that we have what we asked of him" (1 John 5:14–15 NIV).

Based on the Scriptures, we can confidently ask of God *anything* in line with His will. Forgiveness is God's will. We know from His Word He *desires* to forgive, therefore we can confidently receive His forgiveness. "If we confess our sins to him, he is faithful and just to forgive us and to cleanse us from every wrong" (1 John 1:9).

Once we have repented, we must *accept* God's forgiveness by faith. In other words, we must *choose to believe* we are forgiven because God will never renege on His Word. What God promises to do, He does.

Forgive Yourself

Even as you fully accept God's forgiveness, take time to forgive yourself. If you've asked God to forgive you for a sin, then you, too, must let it go. Resist opportunities to mentally rehearse your sins. Instead, enjoy the benefits of forgiveness—never take upon yourself the guilt of that sin again. Proclaim, "Jesus paid the price for my sin. I am forgiven! I am cleansed of this. I will walk free of this sin from this moment on!"

Jesus said, "So if the Son sets you free, you will indeed be free" (John 8:36). In other words, if Jesus forgives you, you *are* forgiven! The freedom of forgiveness is an accomplished fact. It is a certainty.

Accept the Fullness of Forgiveness

You may feel as though forgiveness is a topic with which you are already familiar. You are probably right—we've all been taught a great deal about forgiveness. But be careful not to dismiss the topic out of hand, as though it were a bridge you've already crossed. Forgiveness is a daily need, to be received and given as life unfolds. The Lord's Prayer talks about "our daily bread" and "forgive us as we forgive those who trespass against us" almost in the same breath. Without forgiveness, we are doomed to cope with our issues in our own strength; with it we are released, and we release others, from spiritual captivity.

Some people believe their sin is too horrible for God to forgive. That simply isn't true; the sacrifice on the Cross and the power of Jesus' Resurrection are not diminished by anything we can do, no matter how evil. Neither is there any sin bigger than God's desire to forgive us. His goodness is greater, far greater, than any sin we can commit.

What if you've sinned over and over again? Has God grown weary of forgiving you? No! God is patient with us. The Bible tells us Jesus "understands our weaknesses, for he faced all of the same temptations we do" (Heb. 4:15).

One day, Jesus' disciples came to Him and asked, "How many times should we forgive someone?" Jesus responded, "Seventy times seven." What exactly does that mean? Are we to count the number of times someone sins against us? No. In simple language Jesus was commanding His followers to forgive *the same way God forgives us:* as often as necessary.

When we forgive people "seventy times seven," we are releasing them from our clutches so God can totally invade every area of their lives with His perfect love. We are putting those people, and ourselves, into a position to be healed and made whole, from the inside out.

Trust God to forgive *fully, perfectly, and in every area of life.* Ask God to help you to forgive others as He forgives. The more you forgive others, the more your joy will increase.

RECEIVE GOD'S AMAZING LOVE

Think about the love you felt when you first held your child in your arms.

Think about the love you felt when someone you thought you lost forever suddenly found you again.

Those feelings of love are likely to be inseparable from great feelings of joy.

In order to experience *abiding* joy, we must have a prevailing sense of abiding love. Only God can give such love.

God's love is truly amazing. He loves because it is His nature to love. He loves us even when we sin. He loves us because He made us. He loves us to the degree He sent Jesus to take on our sin and become the sacrifice for it, so we could be forgiven and live with God forever. Jesus said of His own sacrificial death, "There's no greater love than to die so that others might live" (see John 15:13).

The world rarely applauds God's unconditional, unceasing love. Instead, God is portrayed as a stern taskmaster who disapproves of pleasure and prosperity. God is widely misunderstood, largely unknown, and often conveniently marginalized in order to still the voice of the conscience.

It is up to us to *remind ourselves* of God's unending love. Keep close to your heart the words of 1 John 4:16 and speak them often to your own spirit: "We know how much God loves us, and we have put our trust in him."

Dwell on Romans 8:1 and recite it aloud: "There is no condemnation for those who belong to Christ Jesus."

Cling to the message of 1 John 4:4, which is a verse not only about the Holy Spirit in you, but the power of the Holy Spirit's love: "Greater is he that is in you, than he that is in the world" (KJV). God's ability to love you is greater, far greater, than any power the world has to love or condemn.

BECOME A FOUNTAIN OF JOY TO OTHERS

The joyful person is a delight to be around, one who spreads joy wherever he or she goes. When you're in the company of joyful people, you get the sense they can do *anything*. In fact, when you spend time with those who exude joy, you begin to believe *you* can do anything!

Note what Isaiah says to the joyful person:

> You will go out in joy
> and be led forth in peace;
> the mountains and hills
> will burst into song before you,
> and all the trees of the field
> will clap their hands. (Isaiah 55:12 NIV)

In other words, for the joyful person, the world turns cheerful. Read that verse again. Can you see the colors brighten and hear the music swell? The joyful person doesn't see the world through rose-colored glasses. The world really *is* rose-colored to the joyful person!

Have you noticed that when you are joyful, you feel up to every task? Instead of feeling as if you are swimming upstream, you feel yourself coasting downhill with the breeze in your face and a song in your heart.

Joy, in other words, changes a person's perspective.

You are thankful for being forgiven and you have compassion for those who are hurting. You are free and you forgive others *freely*.

When you know you are loved, love pours out of your heart. You want others to know God.

Imagine living without joy. The atmosphere of every day would be gloom, doom, depression, despair, sadness, sorrow, and grief. The world would wax dull and grey. That is what it is like to live under a curse.

Joy is what God desires, and what He freely offers. Receive it! Choose to see the world through the sparkling lens of joy. Teach your children to see things in a positive light. Their awareness of God's blessings, and their ability to bless others, will increase.

Insight from Marilyn

I remember returning from a long overseas ministry trip not too long ago. The trip was exciting, productive, and completely joyful. Our ministry team witnessed amazing things. Our hearts were filled to the brim with thanksgiving and praise for what happened—the souls saved, the sick healed, the miracles performed. Did we ever rejoice!

When I arrived home, my husband, Wally, was excited to see me. He gave me a warm, wonderful greeting and asked me to tell him all about the trip.

Well, you'd never know I was full of joy, because, at that moment, all I wanted were a bath and my bed—and I said as much. You can imagine how my husband felt. He was so cheerful and eager to hear about my trip, and I acted as if it was just too much trouble.

Yes, after my long journey, I needed rest and a good night's sleep in my own bed, but I could have handled that special time more thoughtfully. It was a prime opportunity to experience pure joy with my husband, and I almost missed it. Thankfully, God helped me to adjust my attitude. I shared the details of the trip and Wally and I rejoiced in God's goodness *together*.

Tap into joy. It will give you the strength to deal with every family situation!

* * *

Make joy the currency of your home. Are you cheerful at work and cranky at home? After a long day at the office, does your family get the leftovers of your love?

Before you walk in the door, look to God for help in tuning up your attitude. The events of the day may have drained your emotions and sapped your strength. You may long to climb into your pajamas and stare vacantly at the TV. But, if you'll *choose* to brush off the effects of a hard day and spend quality time with your loved ones, you will be refreshed and rejuvenated.

Enjoy your loved ones for who they are rather than who you want them to be. Laugh with your kids. Don't allow your foibles or the flaws of others to inhibit or embarrass you. Laugh about them. Teach your children that some things in life are just plain *funny*, and laugh heartily *together*.

Forgive your children freely. Teach them to forgive quickly and completely.

Shower affection upon your children. Welcome their displays of affection in return.

The child who is free of condemnation and who is sheltered by love is a joyful child. A family in which forgiveness and affection flow freely is a joyful family. Such a child and such a family are truly *blessed*!

POWER POINT

Nehemiah 8:10 says, "The joy of the Lord is your strength!" This is the strength that puts us over the top in life. It is the spiritual fuel of victory! Guard your joy by forgiving freely. Your family will benefit and your children will prosper.

13

Go for the Extreme Harvest

Everybody I know loves harvesttime.

We love days marked by accomplishment, by acknowledgment, by reward.

We love crossing the finish line, completing the course, graduating with honors.

We love days of celebrating the abundance of "good fruit" produced in our lives.

Fruitfulness is the Bible word referring to the bearing of good things. The term can refer to the bearing of children. It can refer to the production of crops. It can refer to the way in which we develop character, especially the "fruit of the Spirit" (see Galatians 5:22–23).

The prophet Isaiah said that the life of a blessed person is like the earth that experiences the outpouring of God's rain upon it. The rains make the parched soil "bring forth and bud, that it may give seed to the sower, and bread to the eater" (Isa.

55:10 KJV). What a wonderful illustration of the fruitfulness God gives as a blessing to our lives.

Hallmark of Blessing #7:
Extreme Fruitfulness

Fruitfulness is a *process*. It doesn't happen overnight. Fruitfulness happens over time, as a result of things we learn, things we do, and things we allow God to do. The process of fruitfulness, whether in nature, our individual lives, or in our generations, involves seed planting, cultivation, and pruning. Once the seed is planted, however, the landscape of your life is subject to change.

TURN YOUR FIELD INTO YIELD

Turning a generational curse into a generational blessing begins in just a moment of time. It starts to happen the instant we *plant our faith* to believe God for something better, and then begin to plant seeds of new Bible-based thoughts, God honoring feelings, and Spirit-led behaviors with the potential to produce a full harvest of blessing. The full reversal of a generational curse, and the creation of a generational blessing occur as we cultivate and nurture the seeds we've planted.

Insight from Sarah

One of my favorite harvest stories is about a farmer who experienced a devastating year back in the 1970s. Weather conditions ruined his crops. As he walked his acreage one day, he saw a strong soybean plant standing somewhat isolated from the other vegetation. He went over to this plant and picked off the pods: 202 of them. He opened each pod and took out a total of 503 soybeans. He dried these beans over the winter and planted them the next spring. He harvested thirty-two pounds of soybeans the next fall, and he again took all the beans out of the pods and dried them over the winter.

The following year the farmer planted an acre of soybeans using those 32 pounds of seed from which he harvested 2,409 pounds of soybeans. In the fourth year, he harvested 2,100 *bushels* of soybeans and cashed them out for $15,000. In four years, he produced 2,100 bushels from an original 503 beans. That is *fruitfulness!*

What might *you* plant? As with the soybean farmer, your seed packet may be small, but it is packed to the brim with life. What are your hopes and dreams for your family? Ask God what seed you can plant and do it! The tiniest seed contains the makings of a great harvest and your family's growing season can start today.

Seed planting might take a day or two, if the weather is right and the soil has been prepared. The actual harvest of a crop is also usually accomplished in a matter of days. The *cultivating* process is longer and more painstaking but, without it, the potential of your seed is compromised.

The season of cultivation is not the time to drop your guard. Though the seed and the soil are doing the work of growing your crop, a good farmer is vigilant, giving careful attention to the condition of the new growth so adjustments can be made as needed.

The same is true in our lives and in the lives of our children. Just as we are continually planting, we must continually check for growth by asking ourselves: *Are we moving in the desired direction? Are we growing stronger spiritually? Are our children confident and secure? Is our interaction godly? What adjustments can we make to produce a harvest of blessing that can be passed down to the next generation?*

Growth Spurts and Setbacks

We are works in progress: our faith is developing, we and our loved ones are maturing, our understanding of God's ways is increasing. Ideally, our overall growth, though incremental, remains steady. Realistically, however, most of us can identify spurts of rapid growth, seasons of all-out harvest where everything seems to be working. And if we're honest, there are also periods where we feel stymied, times when we see no fruit, no progress.

Every season plays a role in our development as individuals and as a family. Solomon spoke eloquently about the harmony of the seasons:

> To everything there is a season,
> A time for every purpose under heaven:
> A time to be born,
> And a time to die;
> A time to plant,
> And a time to pluck what is planted.
> (Ecclesiastes 3:1–2 NKJV)

Ironically, some of our best progress results from the difficult seasons of life, the days of tedious cultivation when our methods seem to produce diminishing returns or unexpected circumstances drain our energy and resources.

In 1996, cyclist Lance Armstrong received devastating news: he was suffering from testicular cancer that had already spread to his lungs and brain. In the blink of an eye, he was sidelined. Every goal was on hold, every dream in question. Worse, he was given less than a fifty-fifty chance to recover. His body, and his world—including his cycling career—were falling apart. In the midst of the mayhem, survival became the priority.

The rest is history. Armstrong beat the medical odds, got back on the bike, and went on to win the *Tour de France*—seven times! Cancer may have sidelined the athlete for a season, but his personal growth did not cease. Lance Armstrong came back stronger than ever and with a new, expanded vision. Today, he is using the tools sharpened during his illness—optimism, compassion, and relentless perseverance—to improve the lives of cancer patients worldwide. Armstrong's legacy of hope will reach beyond his lifetime, but it began in a grueling season of cultivation.

Use Setbacks as Seed

In nature we see utter destruction overwhelmed by burgeoning life. A few years ago, Colorado suffered its largest-ever forest fire, thirty miles southwest of Denver in the Pike-San Isabel National Forest. The Hayman Fire was neither natural nor an act of God. It was started by an arsonist, a catastrophic event, charring nearly 140,000 acres and destroying 133 homes. Because the burn area was stripped of growth and became resistant to water, the burn area is now prone to flash flooding. Whereas fire was the chief concern, now heavy rains are most feared.

The fire wiped out everything in its path. When it was over, the once-inviting landscape looked forbidding and otherworldly. All signs of life were gone. Yet, somewhere in the burn zone, aspen seeds began to sprout and take root unassisted by conservationists. Somehow, the seeds, packed by God with the potential for new life, survived the devastation and took root in the blackened soil.

Setbacks occur in the life of every individual and every family. The way we handle downturns has a great deal to do with where we end up, individually and generationally. A can-do attitude modeled by parents can become a family trait bearing fruit throughout the family tree. Unfortunately, a defeatist approach can be equally productive.

The key to turning setbacks into successes is, first and foremost, to cling to God and rely on His grace to empower you. God's grace can intervene to reverse a setback, prevent a crop failure, or restore what was lost—even when our mistakes are the cause!

When a setback changes the landscape of your life, trust God to bring new life into the situation. Put yourself, your family, and the crisis in God's hands. Don't run from the challenge; adjust to and learn from it. Look for signs of life springing up in the hard soil and realize that, if you will maximize every opportunity to learn and grow, the trial will become the seed of new growth. In the final analysis, a bad situation can produce a magnificent harvest.

Pruning: Painful but Necessary

A third phase of fruitfulness is *pruning*. Pruning is part of the maturation process in any believer's life. Young sprouts and saplings are not pruned—pruning is for fruit-bearing vines and trees. Increasingly, the Lord seeks to cut away from our lives anything that does not have the mark of eternity on it.

Insight from Marilyn

Wally and I began in the ministry as assistant pastors at a church in Amarillo, Texas. The church provided living quarters for us. The space was small, run-down, and in desperate need of cleaning and a fresh coat of paint.

I was accustomed to living in a nice home and was disappointed with the accommodations. My husband was patient with my complaints. I kept nagging him, saying, "You need to tell the pastor we need a decent place to live!"

Wally wouldn't have it. He said, "God led us here and we're going to be obedient to His call." I decided to help God set things right. I told my husband that if he didn't do something about the situation, I was going home to my mother.

My pouting didn't move Wally, so I made good on my threat and went home to Mother. On the way there, God gave me part of a Scripture verse: "I have set before thee an open door, and no man can shut it" (Rev. 3:8 KJV). I briefly considered the Scripture and continued on my way.

Mother was very gracious during my stay. She baked my favorite pie and talked very sweetly to me. While I was there, one of her friends called to ask for my address in Amarillo. She said she had a Scripture she wanted to send me. Mother told her, "Marilyn is right here—you can tell her now" and handed me the phone.

The woman said, "Marilyn, I don't know what this means, but God said that He has opened a door for you that no man can close."

I finished the pie and went straight back to Amarillo. That was when I really began to teach the Bible. The church had a class for young married couples. They asked me to teach the class, although I was just twenty-six. We started with twenty-two in the group. Within a year, attendance climbed to one hundred! That was the seed of my calling as a teacher. I never knew it could be so fulfilling. And it has become more and more exciting ever since.

Had God not pruned me during that trip to Mother's and in the months after, I would have missed out on the marvelous life He has given me, and the fruit of the past fifty years of ministry would have been someone else's to harvest.

Pruning directs growth to produce premium fruit. What is not healthy or productive is cut away, including any growth that would detract from the quality or quantity of the fruit—and therefore, the harvest. In this way, the energy of the plant is conserved for the development of the very best fruit.

When God prunes away an unproductive activity or particular habit from your life, He is setting you and your loved ones up for blessing. He may show you better ways to spend family time or ask you to curb certain activities or knee-jerk emotional reactions. He may draw you away from certain relationships He knows are counterproductive in some way. Whatever pruning He does will move you closer to the harvest you and He desire.

Pruning can be painful, especially if you take pleasure in something He is asking you to drop. Keep in mind, always, that the Lord is seeking to get your eyes off the flesh and onto those things with eternal value. He prunes away what holds you back from bearing genuine spiritual fruit. In the process of stripping away the unproductive areas of your life, He is creating an environment that will further benefit your children and, one day, your children's children.

Insight from Marilyn

We parents are part of the pruning process in our children's lives. A number of years ago I became very concerned about a friendship Sarah was developing with a young man she met at a coffeehouse. Sarah was still single at the time, living on her own, and I knew she enjoyed this man's company.

As I was praying for Sarah regarding this young man, I realized he was not born again. The Lord also brought James 4:4 to my mind: "Friendship with this world makes you an enemy of God."

I had a very strong conviction this young man wasn't destined to be a good friend for Sarah, but I also knew I needed to trust the Lord to reveal this to her. If there's one thing we as parents must do, it's to love our adult children and trust God to deal with them *directly*.

A short while later, this young man asked Sarah to go away with him for a weekend. Suddenly, Sarah saw him in a new light. He overplayed his hand and his motives for their relationship became very clear to her.

The Lord pruned this man out of Sarah's life in His way, using His methods. Trust God to do that if you see relationships in your child's life that could use some divine pruning.

God's pruning is not designed to limit us but to expand everything good in our lives and to make way for new, healthy growth that will produce better and better fruit. Jesus said, "I am the true vine, and my Father is the gardener. He cuts off every branch that doesn't produce fruit, and he prunes the branches that do bear fruit so they will produce even more" (John 15:1–2).

ANTICIPATE A SUPERNATURAL, GENERATIONAL HARVEST

Be "extreme harvest"-minded. Keep planting and cultivating and remain open to the Father's direction. Then expect Him to bless your life and prosper your children. Don't focus on life's obstacles; keep your eyes fixed on the long-term. Scripture says, "He who observes the wind [and waits for all conditions to be favorable] will not sow, and he who regards the clouds will not reap" (Eccl. 11:4 AMP).

Allow the promise of future results to catapult your thinking beyond the short-term difficulties and disappointments you face. Be like the faithful soybean farmer whose entire crop was reduced to a single healthy plant: take the seed you have available and plant it!

"But," you may be saying to yourself, "I see so little fruit in my life or in my family."

Don't be discouraged. The harvest *will* come. The Bible gives us this tremendous word of encouragement: "Don't get tired of doing what is good. Don't get discouraged and give up, for we will reap a harvest of blessing at the appropriate time" (Gal. 6:9).

POWER POINT

The extreme harvest of generation blessing starts the instant we plant our faith to believe God for something better. Sow the seeds of Bible-based thoughts, God-honoring feelings, and Spirit-led behaviors and you'll produce a godly harvest in your family—nimble minds, healthy emotions, and productive habits.

14

Factor Out Fear

The story is told about a mother and daughter who prepared a meal together for a special gathering of four generations of their family. Quickly, but carefully, the woman
of the house unwrapped a roast and slapped it onto a cutting
board before placing it in a large Dutch oven.

Her daughter watched her every move as she deftly sliced
off the ends of the roast, coated the remainder with herbs and
spices, and centered it in the pan. Puzzled, the daughter asked,
"Mom, why did you cut off the ends of the roast?"

Surprised by the question, the mother explained matter-of-
factly, "Of course you have to cut off the ends of the roast.
That's simply the way it's done."

Unconvinced, the daughter pressed the issue: "Yes, Mother,
but *why* is that the way it has to be done?"

At a loss for words, the mother replied, "That's how
Grandma taught me to prepare a roast. That's just how you
prepare a roast, that's all."

The daughter walked into the family room where the rest of the clan was gathered. She sat on the ottoman next to Grandma's chair and asked, "Grandma, why do you cut off the ends of the roast before placing it in the pan?"

Grandma nodded toward Great-Grandma and said, "Mama told me to cut off the ends and I cut them off."

With a twinkle in her eye, Great-Grandma chuckled and said: "Honestly, dear, didn't you know? I asked you to cut off the ends because the roast was too big for our old roasting tin."

For generations, the women in our fictitious family learned that to cook a good roast, you had to cut off the ends. It was a family tradition but, in the end, it was based on a misunderstanding.

The roast example is a harmless one; it doesn't matter all that much if the roast is carved before it is cooked. Not all cases of misunderstanding or misinformation are critical to the well-being of your generations. However, certain things your children learn will either prepare them for blessing or predispose them to loss.

CLEAR OUT THE WEEDS

Every field, however carefully it is planted, gives way to a few weeds. Early in the growing season, it can be difficult to distinguish tiny weeds from desirable growth. However, the savvy cultivator knows the difference and will uproot the trespassers by the right method at the right time. He knows the key to a healthy field is a balanced approach: don't let the weeds choke out the harvest, but don't pull out your seed with your weeds, either.

Spiritually speaking, weeds come in all shapes and sizes. They have this in common: every weed will suck vital nutrition and moisture from the soil, compromising the future of your good seed. And every weed, left untended, will multiply until it overruns your crop.

So if a farmer does everything else right—the best seed, the right crop rotation, adequate moisture, top-grade fertilizer, and perfect timing—but doesn't control which seed takes root, he or she will suffer loss and all the hard work and expense will have been for naught.

Spiritual weeds produce similar damage. You work hard to do the right things; you invest faithfully in the lives of your children. But if you don't recognize the weeds in your spiritual field, or if you ignore the weeds you know are growing there, the wrong crop is sure to come up . . . and the weeds will find their way into future generations.

These weeds have names like: *strife, unforgiveness, selfishness, slothfulness, anger, jealousy,* and *unfaithfulness.* The list goes on. Yet, perhaps the greatest enemy of our souls, and the greatest seed-killer, is *fear.* In one way or another, fear has been at the heart of every sin since the Garden of Eden: "The fruit looked so fresh and delicious, and it would make [Eve] so wise! So she ate some of the fruit. She also gave some to her husband, who was with her. Then he ate it, too" (Gen. 3:6).

When Satan told Eve that eating the fruit would give her knowledge, she was *afraid* to miss out. Satan was cunning—he still is. When he tempts us, he does so by creating in our minds a perceived need. He dangles the bait before us; if we take the bait, it is because he has deceived us into believing we *must have* the thing he is offering.

How does this tie in to your generations? Remember the way sin and iniquity produce the curse. Your weaknesses, your failings can become the struggles faced by the next generation. We can see this in American history, where families, communities, and regions saw racial hatred perpetuated for hundreds of years. For some, the curse continues unhindered and hate crimes result. Racial discrimination is fear-based and the fear is passed from generation to generation. So are the negative results of living under this dreadful curse.

THE HIGH COST OF FEAR

Even those we believe to be brave and powerful can be tormented by fear. King Saul was chosen by God to lead Israel, yet he suffered a lifetime of fear and intimidation. Saul's fear was demonstrated in his words and through a series of disobedient acts that undermined his life and left a deposit of destruction for his generations.

Let's examine three ways fear uproots the seeds of blessing in the lives of God's people.

1. Fear Perverts Your Past.

Fear takes what was once pristine and corrupts it. Fear distorts the memory, unravels past good works, destroys once-honorable reputations, and steals a person's God-given vision.

When God sent Samuel to anoint Saul king, it was clear God had an amazing plan for Saul and his generations. Samuel told Saul, "I am here to tell you that *you and your family are the focus of all Israel's hopes*" (1 Sam. 9:20, emphasis added). What a ringing endorsement, and straight from heaven! Yet, within himself Saul felt unable to measure up and replied: "But I'm only from Benjamin, the smallest tribe in Israel, and my family is the least important of all the families of that tribe! Why are you talking like this to me?" (1 Sam. 9:21).

Although Saul would accept the mantle of king, he was fearful and insecure. From the beginning, Saul discounted God's vision and undermined the legacy of his family.

Insight from Sarah

Reece and I took our children up to the mountains with some extended family. It was a terrific time in a beautiful setting. There was a swimming pool with a fantastic two-story slide, which our daughter and our younger son really enjoyed. However, our son David avoided the slide. Something about it scared him and so, instead of trying it out, he opted to withdraw.

There are times when children need help working through or confronting fear. Reece and I decided this was one of those times. Reece went up to the top of the slide with David. I stood ready at the bottom, where I could catch him. The first run was great. Down he came, right into my arms. He was all smiles. So he wouldn't think one good experience was a fluke, we encouraged a second ride. Run number two was even better. David's confidence was soaring and he was having fun. The third ride didn't go as well. David got turned around on the way down and, although I caught him, he got lots of water in his face. His confidence fell and the fear returned.

We didn't want the experience to end on a bad note, so we pressed for a fourth ride, which went very well. Though three out of four experiences on the waterslide were positive, ride number three governed his memory and distorted what was overall a breakthrough event. To this day, David will tell you he doesn't like waterslides.

Fear begins with a seed. How many fear seeds are you comfortable leaving in the soil of your child's heart? Although we can't peer into the details of Saul's childhood, his behavior reveals the distorted perceptions that had become embedded in his thinking. As a result, this formidable man,

Israel's chosen king, lived in an emotional straightjacket for a lifetime.

2. Fear Paralyzes Your Present.
When Samuel called the people together at Mizpah to select Saul as king, the prophet knew whom God had chosen. The community also proclaimed its support. Yet even this public display failed to make Saul feel accepted.

> *And finally Saul son of Kish was chosen from among them. But when they looked for him, he had disappeared! So they asked the LORD, "Where is he?"*
>
> *And the LORD replied, "He is hiding among the baggage." So they found him and brought him out, and he stood head and shoulders above anyone else. (1 Samuel 10:21–23, emphasis added)*

Imagine God's chosen king cowering in the background, hiding among the baggage. At the very moment in which God promoted him to the highest position in all Israel, Saul was paralyzed by fear.

Unchecked fear will cause you to freeze at key moments, preventing you from living fully in the now and causing you to miss opportunities that may very well be the answers to your prayers for you and your family.

3. Fear "Fades" Your Future.
When Saul and his army gathered at Gilgal to face the Philistines in battle, the enemy amassed an overwhelming force and terrified the Israelites. Saul was obediently waiting for Samuel's arrival to offer the appropriate sacrifices, but as his troops scattered, Saul became fearful. He was afraid that if he waited for Samuel any longer, all his troops would desert him. So Saul

offered the sacrifices himself. Just as he finished, Samuel arrived and said:

> *You have disobeyed the command of the* LORD *your*
> *God. Had you obeyed,* the LORD would have established your kingdom over Israel forever. But now your
> dynasty must end, *for the* LORD *has sought out a man*
> *after his own heart. The* LORD *has already chosen him*
> *to be king over his people, for you have not obeyed the*
> LORD's *command. (1 Samuel 13:13–14, emphasis added)*

One of the most insidious aspects of fear is its ability to reach into your future and strip away what God has already ordained. Although we might not be kings or queens of nations, our futures, and our families' destinies, are important to God and His plan for the earth.

Insight from Marilyn

Over the years, we have ministered in Pakistan five times. I love the Muslim people and experience great joy when I am in their midst.

Particularly since September 11, 2001, the security challenges in traveling to places like Pakistan and Indonesia have increased. Many well-meaning people advised me to avoid these nations long before the September 11 attacks, but each time, God assured me I was to go.

During our most recent mission to Pakistan, the authorities uncovered a terror cell that had targeted me and was planning an attack during our meetings. During our previous visit, these meetings drew hundreds of thousands of people. Fearing an international incident and a horrific slaughter, the authorities withdrew the permit for our venue, a cricket stadium.

We had many opportunities to fear. When we realized we were in danger personally, we could have chosen to flee. Believe me, we were not trying to be heroes and I'm not advocating foolishness. If God says, "Leave!" you must obey Him. But God did not prompt us to leave. Therefore, we stayed.

We had advertised our healing meetings extensively. Many were en route from outside the city, and there was no venue! Fear tried to grip our souls, but we resisted it. We asked our team in the United States to pray. Just in time, we received an invitation from a Catholic church to hold our meetings on its campus. It was a wonderful time of ministry. Although the campus could not accommodate hundreds of thousands, many miraculous healings and salvations occurred.

I was disappointed we were not able to reach as many souls as we hoped, but we left Pakistan thankful for all God did. And He soon blessed us with more when the Pakistani network with whom we have worked for many years invited me to preach at a healing meeting they organized—in Bahrain! This was an answer to my prayers. Our ability to reach Muslims was not diminished by the terror plot. Instead, it was expanding to a nation in which I had no contacts of my own.

The meetings in Bahrain were fabulous and more will come from that precious ministry seed. Had we allowed the fear of danger or our disappointment in Pakistan to discourage our work in the Islamic world, we would have missed this amazing new opportunity to deposit the gospel in Bahrain's thirsty spiritual soil. Now, it will bear fruit there for generations to come.

If we will blow off our insecure moments, learn to push past existing patterns of fear, and embrace every opportunity wholeheartedly, we will find the emotional risk we take is insignificant when compared to the benefits we receive. If we will model this behavior for our children, they will become a can-do generation that truly believes and acts on the biblical truth that "with God all things are possible" (Matt. 19:26 NIV).

Hallmark of Blessing #8
Prevailing Peace

"For you shall go out with joy, and be led out with peace" (Isa. 55:12 NKJV). Where peace reigns, God's presence and blessing are evident and fear is overwhelmed. His Word assures us that, regardless of the circumstances, we can remain embedded in the surpassing peace of God: "Be anxious for nothing, but in everything by prayer and supplication, with thanksgiving, let your requests be made known to God; and the peace of God, which surpasses all understanding, will guard your hearts and minds through Christ Jesus" (Phil. 4:6–7 NKJV).

BE ANXIOUS FOR NOTHING
The apostle Paul gave this command regarding a life of peace. To be "anxious for nothing" doesn't mean you don't care about anything. It means you don't *worry* about anything. Worry is the trademark of fear. Be assured of this: God does not want you to live in bondage to a spirit of fear. Rather, His gift to you is "power," "love," and "a sound mind" (2 Tim. 1:7 NKJV).

How can we resist fear? Begin by making a quality decision to attack fear before it attacks you. Then consider three practical steps.

1. Identify Fears.

Ask God to reveal what situations cause you to flee and what safety zones you run to. Until you look fear dead in the eye, it will continue to taunt you. Do you avoid healthy confrontation by tolerating the inappropriate actions of others? Do you freeze rather than face the music during financial challenges, hoping the problems will magically disappear? Does intimidation keep you from accomplishing what God has promised to help you do? Identify your weak spots and, with God's help, confront them.

2. Find the Root.

Ask God to reveal the root of your fear. Look beyond the surface until you find what drives your fearful tendencies. Avoidance strategies are symptoms. Anger and combativeness are symptoms. Depression is a symptom. Get to the bottom of your issues and keep digging until you have rooted out the painful memories that inform your habitual behaviors. Don't run from your fear. Instead, yank it from the soil of your heart by meditating and speaking God's Word and holding yourself accountable to it.

3. Allow God's Love and Grace to Carry You Beyond Fear.

Once you have identified fearful behaviors and found the root causes, rely on steady doses of God's Word to keep your mind renewed. Keep seeking God in prayer and receive His grace to modify your behaviors. In time, fear will be forced to release its grip on your life. Your example will en-*courage* and empower your children to establish fear*less* lives.

Insight from Sarah

You know the story of our older son, David, and his fear of the waterslide. As a toddler, David was fearful of other situations involving heights, too. Reece and I not only worked with David regarding these fears, we also prayed about the situation. Eventually, we began to call him "Dave the Brave." Today, he is fearless. He was our first child to climb a tree, and sometimes he wants to explore such heights that Reece and I have to resist being fearful!

Benji, Dave's younger brother, is also utterly fearless. That may be his nature, but it also may be the result of watching his older brother, "Dave the Brave," do fairly daring feats.

What I have learned from watching my sons is that it is important not to validate your children's fears. Give them a brave, courageous nickname! See what an impact this can have.

We tend to adopt the fear level of others around us. If you have fear, your children will show fear. If an older sibling is fearful, a younger sibling is likely to be more fearful.

Fear is contagious, but so is faith. Respond to your fears and to the fears of your children with statements of faith. You just might be surprised at how brave *you* become.

The Relationship between Fear and Generational Curses

It is important to identify generational curses so you can take action to reverse them. It is *never* helpful or healthful to *dwell* on those curses. If you allow yourself to become preoccupied with generational curses, you will live with an undercurrent of fear in your soul. You'll always be waiting for the other shoe to drop, the next failure to come, or the next tragedy to surface. That's not what God desires for you. He wants you to leave generational curses behind . . . and move forward to a life of blessing.

Think forward, in faith.

Speak forward, in faith.

Act forward, in faith.

Pray about your concerns and then *move forward* with faith. Trust God to impart His power, His love, and His wisdom.

DIVINE INTERRUPTION

To think forward in faith, keep your focus on God's plan for you and your family.

To speak forward in faith, find Scriptures like Psalm 103:2–4, 2 Timothy 1:7, Psalms 91, Luke 6:38, and Deuteronomy 28:13 that speak to the vision He has given you and pray those verses daily.

To act forward in faith, take one step toward the vision each day. However insignificant that step may seem to be, you'll be headed in the right direction.

15

Reach Beyond Your Four Walls

ook at the world around you. It is the bigger picture in which your land exists. Inside the confines of your home, you set the tone, you establish the guidelines, you decide what comes in and what stays out. But your home doesn't exist in a vacuum, nor should it. Because we are God's people, we are not *of this world*, but by His design, we live *in this world*. We are salt and light, the remnant called to shine the gospel into the hearts of those living in darkness. We are a generation called to bring blessing to the *next* generation, just as Abraham did thousands of years ago.

To bless our world, we must be familiar with the world's needs. We must ask ourselves: *Where is our culture headed? What is the spiritual climate of our city? How do people communicate in our rapid-fire society? Who is influencing whom? What is God's plan and what are the enemy's tactics? How can I share the gospel in a real-world, real-time manner?*

These are the questions asked by world-changers since the

early days of the church. In the first few centuries after Jesus walked the earth, Christianity grew rapidly, despite intense persecution. By the fourth century AD, approximately 10 percent of Constantine's empire was Christian. That's amazing! It's especially remarkable given the fact that, just prior to Constantine's time, every Christian lived with a virtual target painted on his or her back.

What fueled this explosive growth? Tenacity. Early Christians were willing to die for their faith, and they *did*. In the very worst of circumstances—intense persecution, slaughter, and poverty—they reflected God's goodness. They loved one another, they shared the gospel, they gave out of their lack, and they refused to compromise or water down the truth of God's Word. Instead they upheld God's standards and, as persecution forced them far afield, they spread His Word to distant lands.

Two thousand years later, the role of the believer is virtually unchanged. Today *we are the ones* privileged to cover the earth with God's Word and His glory.

SNAPSHOT OF A HURTING WORLD

In some parts of the world, Christianity is still flourishing. As in centuries past, the growth is often greatest where the persecution seems strongest. Sadly, the trend in the United States and much of the Western world is quite the opposite. The U.S. statistics we gleaned from www.battlecry.com are alarming.

The following figures reveal the percentages of those in four age groups who consider themselves to be Bible-believing Christians:

- *Sixty-five percent* of those born between 1910 and 1946
- *Thirty-five percent* of those born between 1946 and 1964

- *Fifteen percent* of those born between 1965 and 1976
- *Four percent* (projected) of those born after 1977 (are or will be Bible-believing Christians).

From sixty-five . . . to thirty-five . . . to fifteen . . . to four percent! If you study any living creature—animal or plant—a trend like that raises fears of extinction.

Perhaps the most telling statistic is the final one. Those born after 1977 comprise an enormous demographic—in the scores of millions of people—and if the projection holds, a staggering ninety-six percent will live without a Bible-based faith in Jesus Christ, making them the *least reached* portion of our population.

Perhaps we should not be surprised. Teens in the United States have been raised without a sound frame of reference for who God is and what it means to have a relationship with Him through Jesus Christ. They tend to consider any mention of God from a worldview of *relativism*, the belief that absolute truth does not exist. Their beliefs are pegged to shifting values. Whatever works in a situation, whatever the media dictate, whatever feels right to the individual, whatever mollifies the conscience is the "right" answer. It is telling that 53 percent of teenagers believe that Jesus sinned. Even more, 65 percent, believe there is no way to tell which religion is "real" (www.battlefield.com).

The enchantments of our world and the media age have led this generation to the brink of ruin. Hollywood, the music industry, Madison Avenue, and the media are selling something. Whether it is a lifestyle, a product, or a secular worldview, the mainstream typically runs contrary to God. The statistics (at www.battlecry.com/casualties.php) reveal the chilling effects of a godless culture on our young people:

- One in four use illegal drugs.
- Half have been drunk in the last month.
- One million teenage girls are pregnant.
- Every year, about 340,000 teenage girls have an abortion.
- Every day, eight thousand contract a sexually transmitted disease.
- Nine out of ten have seen pornography on their computers, and the average teenager will see fourteen thousand sexual images on his television set this year.
- One in ten have been raped.
- One in five have attempted suicide, and more than fifteen hundred succeed in their attempts each year.
- Forty percent have inflicted injury on themselves.
- Forty-three percent believe truth is relative—there are no absolutes.
- Most believe that satisfaction in life comes from pleasure, from things, and from peer approval.

This is a bleak snapshot of a hurting generation. Yet, as grim as the situation is, it is chock-full of opportunities to meet needs. What is your part? If you look closely you will find that wherever you see great emptiness and pain, there is the prospect of offering substance and relief—and you are part of God's solution.

We *must* be proactive. Left to their own devices, young people will take the path of least resistance. They will latch on to society's quick fixes, including sex, money, and recognition, when what they desperately *need*, and what they deeply desire, is an encounter with God. Today's youth are a generation ripe for a divine interruption.

THE POWER OF A DIVINE INTERRUPTION

This is a generation at risk, but not out of reach. Throughout history, God has always stretched out His hand to people in dire straits. Perhaps you can remember a specific moment when God interrupted your path and made Himself known to you, a day when your world stopped and your life was transformed in the blink of an eye. Such an encounter with God gets our attention like nothing else, and He can do it in the most unusual ways.

Insight from Sarah

Especially since Reece and I started a family, God has gripped my soul with a hunger to do all I can to spread the truth of generation blessing beyond the Bowling family's four walls, and beyond Orchard Road Christian Center's walls, to a world that is literally *dying* for truth.

As I mentioned in the introduction to this book, I believe with every cell of my being in the power of a divine interruption from God. I experienced such a moment in my own life, a time when God grabbed hold of me and rattled my cage. In an instant, He positioned me—spirit, soul, and body—on a new path, in a deeper relationship with Him.

Moses had a divine interruption. Imagine God speaking to a man from a burning bush! It was a sudden, unexpected, powerful experience—a few unforgettable minutes that changed Moses' entire life.

Yet God didn't interrupt Moses solely for Moses' sake. While He lifted Moses out from forty years of exile in the wilderness, God was also preparing him to rescue a nation from four hundred years of slavery. What God did in Moses' heart ultimately transformed Israel and changed world history.

God can do the same today, through people like you and families like yours. Ask Him to show you everyday ways to be part of rescuing a generation. Don't dismiss the little things He might ask of you and don't shrink back from the bigger steps He might ask you to take.

Whatever He shows you is *your part,* and *nobody can do it better than you*! It might be as simple as carrying in your wallet the photo of a certain young person as a reminder to pray for him or her, or becoming involved in a youth mentoring organization or ministry at a juvenile detention center. It might be as simple as extending an invitation or giving a young person a special book about a topic you know interests him or her, or offering a single parent a much-needed break by minding his or her child for the afternoon.

God alone knows *fully* how to reach people in powerful and effective ways. Allow the Holy Spirit to help you pray for the next generation. You may not see all your prayers are accomplishing, but never give up. Your prayers pave the way for the gospel to be preached and to be *heard.* And when the gospel is accompanied by love, compassion, and power, the gospel is *received.*

Insight from Marilyn

A couple we know is having a tremendous impact on people in their circle of influence, simply because they are obeying God's voice. They pray for the sick, host a small group, preach the gospel at every opportunity, and they care for somebody else's little boy.

They saw this nine-year-old in great need and they did something about it. His mother is a drug addict unable to give her son the love and respect he needs and deserves. As a result, he struggles with a wide variety of issues, including stealing, lying, and other antisocial behaviors.

Because of his aggressive and sometimes violent tendencies, no one wants anything to do with the child. Kids don't like him and parents don't want him around their children, and all for very good reasons.

Yet God called this couple to intercede by becoming part of this child's world. God prompted them to open their arms and their home to him. They have taken on an enormous responsibility. They have also positioned themselves to be part of God's plan of blessing for this young life. Surely God is using this husband and wife to interrupt the boy's twisted path and turn him back to the God who holds the promise for his future.

GIVE BIRTH TO SPIRITUAL CHILDREN

Not every Christian will become a natural or adoptive parent and many believers are unable to take a needy child into their homes. But every Christian has something to give. Therefore, nobody is beyond *spiritual* child-bearing years. The child you pray for, the teenager who spends time with your family, or the troubled youth next door is within easy reach of the gospel *through you*. Simply put, your spiritual children are all those you influence for Christ, by whatever means.

Insight from Sarah

When I was in my teens, a woman in our church was led by God to pray for me every day. One day this woman asked me if I wanted to get married. At the time, I was so-so about the idea. "Maybe eventually," I said. She pressed a little: "Well, if you did want to get married, what kind of man do you believe you'd want to marry?" I thought about it and listed a few things. She took me seriously and began to pray over my list faithfully.

After I was engaged to Reece, this woman brought the list back to me. She said, "This is what I've been praying for. Let's take a look at this and see if Reece matches up to this list." I read through the list and couldn't help but respond, "Holy cow! He does!"

I was astounded at two things. First, this woman was faithful to pray for me *all those years*. Second, God was so strategic in answering her prayers!

Now, at least partly due to this woman's intercession, I have been blessed with an *amazing* husband. He is the exact right man for me. Reece and I enjoy raising our kids and are blessed to pastor a congregation that is serious about reaching our community and the world. I am completely humbled by God's radical goodness—and by the wonderful ways He uses people to touch our lives.

Spiritual parenthood springs from a heart of obedience to do whatever God asks. Few people have heard of Mordecai Ham. He was a Baptist evangelist in the early twentieth century who preached crusades and revival meetings across the South. He was raised in Kentucky and his father and grandfather were pastors. He had a rich heritage of Christian faith and a conviction that he needed to reach young people with the gospel.

In 1934, Mordecai Ham preached a revival service in North Carolina. When he gave the altar call, a sixteen-year-old responded to the invitation to receive Jesus as his Savior. The boy's name was Billy Graham.

You don't know who in your Sunday school class of three-year-olds may turn out to be the next world-famous evangelist. You don't know who in the youth group you help lead might have an impact for Christ in your city or your state. You don't know who in the group of young women you chaperone at summer camp might one day become a missionary who will be the catalyst for an entire tribe to accept Jesus Christ.

Be faithful to sow the Word in the hearts of children and teenagers whenever and wherever you have the opportunity. Trust God to grow the seeds you plant in their lives into a tremendous harvest for the gospel. Make Psalm 89:1 your rallying cry: "With my mouth will I make known Your faithfulness from generation to generation" (AMP).

GET REAL; GET REAL RESULTS

One of the great challenges of modern-day evangelism is to reach teens and young adults in a culturally relevant way. Today's youth receive and process information differently from the baby boomers or any other generation.

In our frenetic technological environment, youth are barraged by messages from every segment of society and every corner of the globe. Since it is often the case that both parents work outside the home, young people have more unsupervised time in which to explore and digest information entering the home via the Internet, television, cell phones, and radio.

Because they have so much information from which to choose, the younger ones have become extremely selective about the messages they are willing to receive. They disdain messages wrapped in packaging they see as being old or out of touch. If you plan to walk up to the average unchurched young person and say, "Jesus loves you," you had better be prepared for your words to be dismissed out of hand. Although it is true Jesus loves that young person, the words don't ring true because they seem trite or clichéd.

Familiarize yourself with the gadgets young people—your own children—are using. The Information Age has created a new, ever-changing communication environment. Today's youth have a unique take on things and a shorter attention span than their parents—about the length of time between commercial breaks on television. If your children own cell phones, you've seen them text their friends in mid-conversation and respond to every blip and bleep that comes across the screen.

Many of the information sources we currently rely upon didn't exist just a few years ago, and certainly not in the numbers available today. Young people know what they want and they know where to find it. All too often, when it comes to the spiritual, it is *not* their parents' brand of faith. For them to consider a relationship with God, they must believe it will transcend the superficiality that surrounds them. God must be seen as real *to them* in their culture, in their time.

To share the gospel with the next generation, it is important to realize that while the authentic captures their attention, today's youth do not consider information in the same linear fashion their parents did. Their approach is more eclectic, pulling a little bit of information from here, and a little bit from there.

When it comes to religion, many young people dabble. They find the parts of Buddhism they think are cool, add some attractive aspects of Hinduism, a pinch of Islam, and a sprinkle of agnosticism for a little more edge. But in the end, this kind of spiritual cocktail fails to satisfy the need for what is real. Many dabblers conclude religion is empty after all, just another waste of time. The spiritual void, however, remains. The "God-shaped hole" demands an answer, and one way or another, it *will* be filled.

You may not always know the right words to say. Don't be discouraged and don't give up. There is too much at stake! You *can* learn to relate to young people. The real key is to *listen*. A young person always responds to an adult who sincerely, consistently, and patiently listens to what he has to say—not with ridicule or condemnation, but with love. Reading off the rules without investing in relationship will produce nothing more than rebellion. Young people will respond to your heart even more than to your words.

Take Your Influence to the World Stage

Did you know that 37 percent of the world's population is under the age of twenty? World evangelism is now a matter of *youth* evangelism, often to those whose circumstances are dismal. Case in point: in Africa, by the year 2020, one out of two young people under the age of eighteen will be orphaned, primarily owing to AIDS and to civil wars.

Insight from Sarah

One of the great blessings my parents have given me is the opportunity to travel. They have modeled for me a passion to know what God is doing in the world. By encouraging me to experience other lands, they have fostered in me a heart for seeing the whole world come to Christ.

Because I was a ministers' kid, I began to travel extensively when I was five. I admit there were times during my youth when I wasn't all that excited about it. But now I look back on my experiences in more than fifty nations and I can see God's perfect design on my life. What an extraordinary blessing, and I am so grateful for it.

Now, as a mom, I'm able to pass that blessing to my children. My six-year-old daughter, Isabell, has already been in fifteen nations; my four-year-old son, David, and three-year-old son, Benji, have each been in ten countries. They are developing a keen awareness of the world and they realize that, everywhere on the planet, there are children with tremendous needs.

As our kids travel, they have opportunities to reach out to others. In their own unique ways, they are able to touch the hearts of other children from other cultures—really, from other worlds.

That is an aspect of generation blessing that absolutely makes my heart soar!

On the world stage, of course, we face the challenge of meeting the physical and material needs of children so they *can hear* the gospel. Before we can address children's spiritual and educational needs, we need to realize that children who are hungry or homeless are not children who have a readiness of heart or mind to go to school or take in spiritual truth. If we will meet their basic needs first, we can reach their hearts in time.

OUR CALL TO "WORLDCHILD"
Our concern for youth is focused through WORLDCHILD, a division of Marilyn Hickey Ministries. (You can read more about this on www.world-child.org.) We believe very strongly

in taking the message of God's love, God's power, and God's Word to the next generation by:

- equipping them with needed resources and materials.
- empowering them with practical training and education.
- encouraging them with meaningful assistance and aid.

As a part of our ministry to youth, we are asking God for new ways to be effective. At present, we partner with John Maxwell and his Million Leader Mandate to conduct leadership training events in nations of the world. It's a massive target and a huge undertaking, but we serve a big God who meets big needs.

One of our target nations for WORLDCHILD is Cambodia. Here's why:

- Fifty-three percent of all the children in Cambodia are malnourished, and one in eight dies before age five, largely due to preventable diseases. [www.asiaweek.com/asiaweek/magazine/99/0917/hospital.html; www.parish-without-borders.net/cditt/cambodia/cb-politics04.html]
- Cambodian children as young as six years of age are prostitutes in the sex trade market, and 35 percent of all prostitutes in that nation are under the age of 16. [www.acr.hrschool.org/mainfile.php/0112/61/].
- Nearly 300,000 children in Cambodia were in danger of losing their parents to AIDS-related illnesses in 2006. [www.diysri.blogspot.com/2006/12/childs-life-with-aids.html].
- A third of the population lives on less than $1 a day. [www.futurecambodiafund.org/generalinfo/cambodiainfo.html]

Facts such as these break our hearts. There's so much to be done, and so much we *must* do.

Providing practical assistance, such as supplying bicycles for orphans and books to create a library at an orphanage, can make a surprising difference. A young person who can get to a job and who can read is a young person with a future—and a young person who can encounter God through His Word.

WORLDCHILD, of course, isn't the only organization offering assistance to children, teens, and young adults. Samaritan's Purse has a powerful impact on children, particularly the poor, sick, and suffering. World Vision is reaching children throughout the world, and especially orphans of the AIDS epidemic in Africa. Mission of Mercy is having a tremendous effect on the next generation by providing for the practical needs and the education of children.

If you want to impact the next generation on a global level, seek out a ministry to the world's youth and get involved. Give what you can and help your children do the same. Go where you can and pray about bringing your children with you. Pray together. You and your children can make a difference! You *can* set in motion a generational blessing that goes far beyond your four walls.

Insight from Marilyn

As I have traveled the world in recent years, I have been impressed by the number of young people who come to our evangelistic and healing meetings. The young people, especially, are eager to learn about Jesus and to learn the truth of God's Word. They have an innocence and an enthusiasm that motivates me to continue. I want to keep traveling and working in ministry as long as I can. There are tens of millions of children and teens yet to be reached, along with millions of their parents, in every area of the world.

We'd be delighted for you to join us in the work of WORLD-CHILD. As Sarah says often, "There's something *everybody* can do!"

DIVINE INTERRUPTION

*B*ecause a high percentage of the U.S. population consists of teens and young adults, what we do or fail to do over the next five years will impact our world for the next five decades. We have been given a tremendous challenge, and an even greater opportunity, to lay a foundation of generation blessing globally! How will you maximize this opportunity?

16

Frame Your Future of Generation Blessing

We believe God's Word and we have our marching orders. We are called to raise strong families, and God has taught us how to do so successfully. We know each of us has something to give to the next generation and we know it is something eternal. We know *we can* do these things. More importantly, we know in our hearts *we must*.

Now it is time to frame the future we desire, the future God has ordained for our generations. We know that without a vision, our beliefs languish and the future passes us by. But when we know where we are headed and we *act upon truth*, we bring God's power to bear upon our circumstances, and the circumstances change.

We are world-changers and difference-makers called to set in motion a legacy, and it begins with our own families.

So, what is your dream for your family?

What are your hopes for your generations?

Which circumstances need to change?

What curses do you want to reverse, and what blessings do you long to see in your family tree?

If you could recreate your world and your family's future—*and you can*—what would it look like?

YOU HAVE THE POWER TO CREATE

We are created in the image and likeness of God. (See Genesis 1:26.) He has given us dominion, the authority to reign on the earth in His name. He *expects* us to use His authority in ways He would use it. We are His *agents of change* in the earth, people of extraordinary creative power, because the Spirit of God lives within us.

Remember, we are to rule and reign over the land He has given us. We have the authority to conform our land to our vision—the vision God has given us. How do we do that? By following God's example. Once again, Pastor Hanes has remarkable insights into our role in changing the world around us.

God Had a Vision for the Universe and He Spoke It Into Being

When God set Creation in motion, the power of His words arrested both chaos and darkness and imposed perfect order: "The earth was empty, a formless mass cloaked in darkness. And the Spirit of God was hovering over its surface. Then God said, 'Let there be light,' and there was light" (Gen. 1:2–3).

From His divine imagination and *with His words*, God created what He desired. He executed His plan for the worlds with precision. Everything He created continues to be held together to this day by the very words He spoke at the beginning: "By faith we understand that the worlds were framed by the word of God, so that the things which are seen were not made of things which are visible" (Heb. 11:3 NKJV).

God moved in absolute, unchallenged authority to frame the world in which we live. With His words He created its geography, function, ecology, boundaries, geology, energy, climate, orbit, tides, and productivity (including minerals, oil, plant life). He methodically created a complete, self-sustaining planet and He placed you and your family on it.

God Has a Vision for Your Family and You Are to Speak It into Being

When God gives you a family and His promises for your family, He is entrusting to you the power and the responsibility to activate His plan.

It is not only in God's power to declare and establish things with His words. He has delegated that power to us. He didn't give this power to the other creatures of the earth. Monkeys, horses, birds, lions—none can rise above the third-dimension plane. All are subject to the whims of nature and the human race. Even the king of the jungle, the majestic lion, with his thick mane and fierce roar, cannot speak something into being.

Only men and women can touch the divine in this way. In fact, we are commanded by God to do so.

OVERCOME YOUR NIGHT SEASONS

To frame your world and to bring it in line with God's vision for your family, you must work to clear your land of the weeds and enemies assigned to overtake your territory.

We don't live in the Garden of Eden. The perfect order that once existed on the earth is gone. We live in a fallen world and we do God's bidding in the face of opposition. Therefore, we succeed in the vision only when we persevere through difficult times.

Though our lives are not idyllic, they are meant to be victorious. When darkness covered the earth, God acted to counteract the darkness by calling light into existence. God saw the light as being good, so "he separated the light from the darkness" (Gen. 1:4).

Then God gave the newly separated darkness a specific name—He called it *night*. (See Genesis 1:5.) Darkness is oppressive and isolating. Before God placed limits on it, darkness was perpetual. But He reigned in the darkness; He gave it a boundary and called the blackness *night*.

Night is temporary. It's a finite "season." Night is not a hopeless time, because the dawn will break and morning will come.

Because you live in a fallen world, you have experienced—or are experiencing at this moment—periods of darkness. When they come, night seasons seem to obliterate the future; they are designed to rob your vision. We tend to put our dreams on hold during our dark times. When light is nowhere to be found, we more easily surrender our creative edge.

Your dark period, whether it is a loss of health, a broken marriage, or a rebellious child, is a season of night. It is *temporary* and it has limits. Your night *will end* and *morning will come*! Plan the end of your darkness by naming it, as God did during Creation.

Joseph named his darkness, too. He was treated unjustly by his own brothers and he was abused in Egypt. Joseph was subjected to a long, dark period. As dark as it was, however, it was temporary and Joseph exited his season of night as a man transformed—powerful and favored by all who knew him.

After suffering the cruelty of an exile imposed by his own

brothers, and during years of separation from his homeland and family, Joseph held his peace. He continued to serve God and he honored those in authority over him, regardless how well or how poorly they treated him.

Joseph's faithfulness before God and men did not go unnoticed. His godly behavior resulted in his promotion by Pharaoh to second in command over all of Egypt. Except with the eyes of faith, Joseph could not have envisioned this glorious outcome when he endured indignity as a slave or suffered unfair imprisonment.

But there came a day when all Joseph suffered, all the inequity he endured, was revealed as a series of divine steppingstones. In that day his brothers sat humbled and desperate before him, fearing their little brother, now among the most powerful men in the world, would exact revenge for the darkness to which they sentenced him.

That is when Joseph named his darkness, saying: "As far as I am concerned, God turned into good what you meant for evil. He brought me to the high position I have today so I could save the lives of many people" (Gen. 50:20).

Joseph asserted his authority over the pain of his past by establishing with his words this truth: the injustice he had suffered was used by God to produce a supernatural outcome: the saving of God's people!

All of Joseph's bitter trials—the abuse of his brothers, his slavery, the false accusations of Potiphar's wife, his abandonment in the dungeon by the cupbearer—were not about him, but about the salvation God planned for Israel.

Name Your Darkness

We name things over which we have authority. If you own a business, you give your business a name. When you give birth or adopt a child, you give your child a name. The act of naming something is a function of your dominion over it.

God created the animal kingdom and, as its Creator, had ultimate authority over it. However, God delegated authority over the earth to Adam. (See Genesis 1:28–29.) Therefore, God instructed Adam to name every creature. In so doing, Adam asserted his authority over the animal kingdom: "The LORD God formed from the soil every kind of animal and bird. He brought them to Adam to see what he would call them, and Adam chose a name for each one. He gave names to all the livestock, birds, and wild animals" (Gen. 2:19–20).

You cannot be subjugated to that which you name. Positionally speaking, that which you name is under you. If you are in the throes of a dark time, name it. If you don't, your darkness will give you a name—it will call you *victim.*

What are you naming your darkness?

What are you calling your disappointments?

What have you named your failures?

Or are they naming you?

Recognize the Prophetic Power of Your Words

Taking authority over your night seasons with your words is not an act designed to provide temporary relief from the pressures of the trials you face. This is a function of your dominion as a believer and it is effective because, as a believer in Jesus Christ, your words are powerful. Jesus said, "I assure you that you can say to this mountain, 'May God lift you up and throw you into the sea,' and your command will be obeyed. All that's required is that you really believe and do not doubt in your heart" (Mark 11:23).

Jesus is so clear about the power of our words that we cannot ignore it. Would God have asked Adam to name the animals if there were no power in doing so? Of course not. God always acts in practical ways to accomplish His purpose. According to His design, those who call Jesus Christ Savior and Lord have been given dominion over this natural world.

Therefore, your words release creative power. Whatever you declare by faith is a prophetic act. Therefore, you must call your night season by a name reflective of God's providential work in your life. This action gives prophetic release to God's intended outcome for your dark season and frames your future with His goodness.

Bear in mind that you must choose your words carefully to *create* what is good and not to *dismantle* it. Remember, Satan desires to devour you and would be happy to use the power of your poorly chosen words to do it. When he suggests you are a victim, assert you are a victor. When he tries to label you a casualty, identify yourself as an overcomer. When he tempts you to be offended, shout out that you have forgiven. When he calls you abandoned, remind him you are a child of the King.

We talked about the devil's predatory nature in earlier chapters. Be alert to his tactics. The enemy will maximize every opportunity to destroy you by whatever means available. He wants to give you a name and then lord it over you. He wants to neutralize your effectiveness and he will ferret out every inroad by which he can accomplish his desire.

See Your Setbacks as Stepping-Stones
In chapter 13, we talked about using your setbacks as seed. That is exactly what you are doing when you name your darkness. Our good friend R. T. Kendall, in his book, *Pure Joy*, calls it "dignifying your trial." To dignify your trial is to become cognizant of the fact that God has wrapped within your time of struggle a purpose to be accomplished. When you see

your trial this way, you are looking beyond the darkness of the situation to find the growth the challenge fosters.

You have heard the expression, "Every cloud has a silver lining." Likewise, every trial is coded with a supernatural outcome. Therefore, every trial or setback can also be seen as a stepping-stone to greater maturity, deeper appreciation, enhanced sensitivity to the things of God, or some other positive development.

Apply These Truths to Your Generations

Everything we have addressed here on a personal or individual level also applies to your family. Your family is part of your God-given territory. You have a heritage and a legacy entrusted to you by God.

- Your family is part of your heritage in God, a gift to be protected and nurtured by you in His name. Name your family's dark times prophetically.
- The blessings you have received through your family tree are part of your heritage. You are the steward of this heritage and you are to pass it on to your generations. Declare your family's heritage and identity in Christ.
- The curses passed down through your ancestors are part of your heritage, too. God has called you to take authority over your family tree and to be an agent of change, one who stands firm to reverse the curse. Speak God's Word to every "mountain" and bring it down.
- You are to create a godly legacy for your descendants by taking ownership and exerting your authority over the territory God has given you. Use the creative power God has invested in you to frame a future of blessing.

Scout Out Your Promised "Land"

We have already acknowledged that God framed the worlds according to His plan. For each of the six days of Creation, God methodically laid out the order of the universe in phases that accomplished His desire. God had a vision in mind. He knew exactly what His massive territory should look like and He knew what it would take to give it life. God has a vision in mind for your generations, a vision of abundant life. He wants to give it to you and He will hold you accountable for it.

Before the Israelites entered the promised land, Moses sent out twelve spies to scout out the land with the following instructions: "See what the land is like and find out whether the people living there are strong or weak, few or many. What kind of land do they live in? Is it good or bad? Do their towns have walls or are they unprotected? How is the soil? Is it fertile or poor? Are there many trees? Enter the land boldly, and bring back samples of the crops you see" (Num. 13:18–20).

Here is some of what the spies reported:

> *"We arrived in the land you sent us to see, and it is indeed a magnificent country—a land flowing with milk and honey. Here is some of its fruit [giant grapes] as proof. But the people living there are powerful, and their cities and towns are fortified and very large."*
> ... *"We can't go up against them! They are stronger than we are!" So they spread discouraging reports about the land among the Israelites: "The land we explored will swallow up any who go to live there. All the people we saw were huge. We even saw giants there, the descendants of Anak. We felt like grasshoppers next to*

them, and that's what we looked like to them!" (Numbers 13:27–28, 31–33)

Ten of the spies offered pessimistic reports. They discounted the positive aspects of the promised land and focused on the challenges: the giants, the fortifications, and their own low self-image. Caleb, for one, had a different approach. "Caleb tried to encourage the people as they stood before Moses. 'Let's go at once to take the land,' he said. 'We can certainly conquer it!'" (Num. 13:30).

How will you respond to the land and the future God has given you? Does fear grip your soul when you see the imperfections in your family or the challenges ahead? Do you feel like Caleb or the ten pessimistic spies? Are you willing to go into your promised land and overcome the giants? Will you harvest your giant grapes or will you shrink back in fear of the challenges and leave your fruit on the vine for someone else to reap?

The ten spies had an *I can't* mind-set, but Caleb had an *I can* spirit. Years later, because he resisted fear and went after the prize, Caleb was rewarded with a choice territory among Israel's tribes.

I can't is a self-limiting statement. *I can* is a spiritual performance enhancer. When you *believe* you can, you can.

With the eyes of your spirit man, peer into the land God has given you and say:

I can raise godly children.
I can be an agent of change in my family and my world.
I can hear God's voice and follow His vision.
I can prevail against the enemies in my land.
I can sow the seeds of generational blessing.

My family can reap the harvest of blessing for all our generations.

PROCLAIM YOUR GENERATIONAL IDENTITY

We mentioned earlier Joel Osteen's teaching, "The Power of Your Bloodline." It is a stunning sermon about generational victory in which Pastor Osteen talks about our identity as children of God.

"He's just got bad blood" is a negative statement referring to a man's natural bloodline, his physical heredity. But natural factors don't have the final word in the lives of spiritual beings. According to 2 Corinthians 5:17, the born-again believer is a "new creation" in whom the old is replaced by the new (NIV). Your natural bloodline is overridden by your spiritual bloodline. Consider your spiritual family tree.

Your Father created everything.
Your Brother defeated Satan.
Your brother David defeated a giant.
Your brother Dan prevailed over lions.
Your brother Moses parted the Red Sea.

You are a spiritual thoroughbred. Winning is in your blood. You and your family members are people of destiny, heirs according to God's promise. No one in your family is an accident. Each of your loved ones is an original. Your family carries the DNA of Almighty God.

Establish and affirm your family's identity in Christ. Look beyond what you see on the outside and affirm what is on the inside: the imprint and the Spirit of God, the heritage of God's covenant people, and a future ordained by the King. You are a spiritual being in whom God has stamped

His eternal plan. Be valiant! Stake out your territory! The King is backing you up.

Insight from Marilyn

Just days before sharing this with you, I had the joy of visiting with a man who took a simple word from God and changed the world for eternity.

Oral Roberts is a dear friend, but he is also a mentor, a man who has served as a model of humility and spiritual authority for our family. I believe that through our family's partnership with his ministry, beginning with my mother in the late 1940s, God has imparted a healing anointing in my life and in Sarah's life. As Psalm 133:2 explains, what is on the head flows down to the body.

During our visit together at Brother Oral's home, he shared with me about the spiritual heritage of his family—seven generations serving God! And they are still serving Him.

It started with Oral's great-great-great-grandfather, who left Wales in the 1700s to settle in America. Seven generations continued in the life of faith in the New World, moving to places like Tuscaloosa, Alabama, and Ada, Oklahoma.

We pick up the story in the twentieth century, when at the age of twelve, Oral became a practicing Methodist. His grandfather, Amos Pleasant Roberts, a lay preacher, died about a year before. "Uncle Pleas," as he was known in town, had a tremendous influence upon young Oral, who loved sitting at his granddad's feet.

Oral's father, Ellis Melvin Roberts, became a preacher and was baptized in the Holy Spirit in 1910, during the Pentecostal movement that swept the nation. He was the first in the Roberts family to be Spirit-filled.

However, it was Oral's mother, Claudius Priscilla Roberts, who moved in the gift of healing and would speak a life of ministry over her son Oral—three years before he was born.

Claudius's healing ministry was well known in town. Whenever people "took sick," they would call for Oral's mother to come out to their farm and minister healing. Three years before Oral's birth, his mother received just such a call. A young farm boy two miles away had pneumonia. Doctors told his family he wouldn't survive the night. They called Claudius and she set out for their farm.

When she reached a barbed-wire fence, Claudius carefully separated the strands of prickly wire so she could climb through. As she did, the wind blew and she sensed the voice of God ready to speak through her. She released this prophetic word: "Lord, if You'll heal this boy, I'll give You my son when he is born."

Three years later, her son was born, but Mama never told him about her promise to God. Ironically, the boy named *Oral* spoke with a stammer. Throughout his childhood, he was ridiculed by his schoolmates. He became fearful of speaking and withdrew from others. Groups of boys would surround and taunt him in the school yard, and when he tried to escape, they would chase him.

One day they chased Oral all the way home, yelling unkind and threatening words. When they reached the house, Claudius came out, shamed the boys for their behavior, and sent them packing. Claudius looked straight into Oral's eyes and told him the story of his calling. She said, "Someday you will preach the gospel. You have the power of God in your life." Then she told her son of the things God would do through him.

Still, challenges lay ahead. Oral dreamed of attending college and law school but saw only poverty all around him. Fearful his ambitions would never come to pass in Ada, he ran away, playing basketball and working multiple jobs to support himself. During a tournament, Oral ran toward the basket, raised the ball to shoot, and collapsed on the court. His coach drove him all the way home. Claudius, who called his name in prayer every midnight since the day he ran away, was thankful her boy was home. Still, she hadn't expected her prayers to be answered in this way.

Oral had advanced tuberculosis. His body quickly became ravaged by the disease. Then the dark day came when the doctors broke the news: they told Oral's parents, Ellis and Claudius, that their son had no more than two weeks to live.

Oral was familiar with his family's history. His maternal grandfather died from tuberculosis at the age of fifty. His mother's older sister also perished from the disease. He reminded his mother of their deaths and said to her, "Well, then, I'm gonna die, too."

But God had another plan. An evangelist named George Munsey came to town and set up a big tent. Oral's older brother, Elmer, decided to take Oral to the meeting. Elmer believed Oral would be healed. He rushed to Oral's bedside and said, "Get up! I've come to take you. There's a man at the tent who's praying for the sick. My wife, Laura, has been there every night and people are being healed. And then I went. And I've come to get you!"

Elmer stretched Oral out in the backseat of the car for the seventeen-mile journey to town. As Elmer's car bumped along the road, the family chattered excitedly.

Suddenly, their voices began to fade and another voice spoke to Oral, saying, "Son, I am going to heal you. You are to take My healing power to your generation and you are to build Me a university based on My authority and the Holy Spirit."

Oral, who had just committed his life to Christ in earnest, had never heard God's voice before. Astonished, he said, "Father, if this is You, say it again."

God repeated His call.

Oral asked again, "Lord, if I'm really hearing You, say it a third time."

Once again, God repeated His words.

When God's voice went still, a "knowing" penetrated Oral's heart—the conviction that everything God said would come to pass. All doubt disappeared; Oral knew when the evangelist touched him, he would be made whole.

When that moment came, Brother Munsey didn't pray the "nice" prayers so many others prayed. Those tired prayers caused Oral's mama to scold them for their faithless words:

"If it's Your will, God."
"Show us, Lord, what Oral has done to bring this sickness upon himself, Lord."
"I pray You'll heal him, God."

No! Brother Munsey reached out his hand to touch Oral and said, "You foul tormenting disease, I command you in the name of Jesus Christ of Nazareth: You come out of this boy. You loose him and let him go free!"

Oral Roberts was healed! His lungs opened and he breathed freely! The evangelist put the microphone to Oral's mouth and Oral's words flowed like a river of praise. The stammering was gone!

Oral Roberts has served God ever since. He took God's healing power to his generation and the generations since. He built Oral Roberts University and founded it on God's authority and His Holy Spirit.

Oral's late wife, Evelyn, served God until her death, and his children and grandchildren are still serving God. The Roberts family has transformed a generation, and many generations to come, with the message that God is good, and God heals.

This legacy of faith began across the Atlantic hundreds of years ago and came to a head when Claudius Priscilla Roberts stood in an open field and spoke a prophetic word that released her son's future. She named the story of Oral's life before he was conceived. Oral's brother Elmer named his sickness "healed." Brother Munsey spoke in the authority of the name of Jesus and ordered the wasting spirit, tuberculosis, to "come out."

The future of the Roberts clan—and the millions they would touch—were framed by anointed words from heaven and a persistent faith in the living God.

Your future is framed the same way—through your prophetic words and your faith. Don't be discouraged by what has always been. Don't be moved by what has not happened yet. See your family's future God's way.

What you see right now as only a glimmer of hope, God sees as a glorious fulfillment.

What you see as a shadow of what might be, God sees in the fullness of eternal reality.

What you see only as the embryo of promise, God sees as an overflowing harvest.

Trust God to work mightily on your behalf.

Trust God to work in every area of your life and in every area of your family life.

Trust God to create a legacy in your family that will bring Him great glory in the generations to come.

DIVINE INTERRUPTION

*D*raw *a line in the sand and name today your family's turning point. Scout out your territory and stake your claim for your family's future, calling it "blessed."*

Proclaim God's will for your lives daily by speaking His Word.

Pray in faith, never quitting. Reign over your land—use your God-given authority to send the devil packing.

Reverse every generational curse by initiating a heritage of blessing. Reach beyond your four walls and change your world by becoming involved in the blessing of others.

Adopt an I must *attitude to frame the future of your generations and fulfill your destiny, in Jesus' name!*

BIBLIOGRAPHY

Hanes, Jack. *The 10 Most Powerful Words You Can Say.*
Sydney: Megalife Ministries, 2007.

Kendall, R.T. *Pure Joy: The Divine Gift That Sings in Our Hearts Even When Things Go Wrong.* Lake Mary, FL: Charisma House, 2006.

Osteen, Joel. *The Power of Your Bloodline.* Houston: Lakewood Church/Joel Osteen Ministries, 2006. Audiocassette.

About the Authors

Marilyn Hickey, the founder and president of Marilyn Hickey Ministries, has been in full-time ministry for more than thirty years. Her ministry specializes in reaching international audiences through television, books, various recorded media, healing meetings, and pastors' and leaders' conferences, as well as Bible and food distribution. Marilyn and her husband, Wallace, founded Orchard Road Christian Center forty-seven years ago. They are the parents of two grown children and live near Denver, Colorado. www.mhmin.org.

Sarah Bowling is the daughter of Pastor Wallace and Marilyn Hickey and is married to Reece Bowling, who serves as the Executive Vice President of Marilyn Hickey Ministries. Together, Reece and Sarah serve as senior pastors at Orchard Road Christian Center. A key focus of Sarah's ministry is "worldchild"—a division of Marilyn Hickey Ministries. Sarah, Reece, and their three children live in the Denver area. www.world-child.org.